The Fred Astaire DANCE BOOK

THE FRED ASTAIRE DANCE STUDIO METHOD

Prepared and Edited by **Lyle Kenyon Engel**

with the assistance of
John Monte, National Dance Director
of the Fred Astaire Dance Studios

Illustrated by **Josh Pryce**

CORNERSTONE LIBRARY • NEW YORK

REPRINTED 1975

CORNERSTONE LIBRARY PUBLICATIONS
Are Distributed By
Simon & Schuster, Inc.
630 Fifth Avenue
New York, N.Y. 10020
Manufactured in the United States of America
under the supervision of
Rolls Offset Printing Co., Inc., N.Y.

Contents

Section One: By Way of Introduction

CHAPTER ONE

The Origin of the Fred Astaire Dance Studios

ONE of the most eloquent tributes ever paid to Fred Astaire was the result of a word-association test given by a psychologist to a group of executive trainees in a large American corporation. Each of the men undergoing the test was instructed to say the first thing that came into his mind upon hearing a certain word. If, for example, the psychologist said "mother," a likely response would be "father." In this particular test, when the psychologist said "dance," a number of trainees immediately said "Fred Astaire"!

Why Fred Astaire's name has come to be synonymous with dancing is not hard to understand. As a musical comedy star, he has entertained capacity audiences on both sides of the Atlantic. As a film star, he has danced in more than thirty motion pictures. In 1958 Fred premiered the first of his spectacular, award-winning television shows. No other dancer has ever been seen, enjoyed and applauded by more people than has this uncompromising craftsman; and no other dancer has so profoundly affected the taste and style of American dance entertainment.

Aside from his pre-eminence as an entertainer, however, Fred has also won recognition as one of the nation's leading proponents of social dancing. He has made the public aware of the beneficial fun to be derived from better ballroom dancing. In order that as many people as possible could participate, the first of the Fred Astaire Dance Studios was founded in 1947 in New York City. The organization has grown to include almost 150 studios in the United States, Canada, Puerto Rico, South America, Australia, New Zealand, Great Britain, and continental Europe.

The master plan for establishing a chain of studios to teach the Astaire style of ballroom dancing was conceived by the late Charles L. Casanave. A well-known motion picture executive and an avid admirer of Fred, Casanave recognized that through a nation-wide and world-wide dance instruction organization Fred Astaire's techniques could be preserved and passed along to the public.

The lessons in this book are based on the proven course of instruction taught at all Fred Astaire Dance Studios. They embody fundamental principles of good dancing, flavored by Fred Astaire's inimitable ease, style and grace. The patterns chosen for each dance are the popular, authentic, and classic steps done on ballroom dance floors today. The elements of correct body movement and styling result in natural, relaxed dancing. The steps have been tailored to the requirements and abilities of every social dancer, for the dance organization's aim is to make the Fred Astaire style of dancing easy and fun for everyone.

"Some people seem to think that good dancers are born," observes Fred, "but all the good dancers I have known are taught or trained. To me dancing has always been fun. I enjoy every minute of it. I am glad that I can now put my knowledge to use in bringing personal confidence and a feeling of achievement to so many people."

As Board Chairman of the Fred Astaire Dance Studios Corporation, Fred devotes a generous portion of his seemingly boundless energy to the task. Serving now as key administrators of the national organization are two sons of the founder: Charles L. Casanave, Jr., President, and Chester F. Casanave, Executive Vice-President.

After fifty-five years in show business—his career having been launched when he was six years old—Fred credits dancing for his unfailing health and youthful appearance.

"Dancing makes you look young," he says. "I mean the very physical act of dancing is almost symbolic of youth. Right now there's no reason why I cannot continue dancing for years. I feel great and I'm dancing well. Dancing keeps me in good shape all year around. I'm limber and active without working at it. I never diet, and I hate calisthenics. They bore me to death."

Dancing is good exercise—it's healthful and it's fun. The more you put into it, the more you will enjoy it. Try it and see for yourself.

CHAPTER TWO

Why Learn to Dance?

DANCING is a natural means of expression. It is almost impossible to listen to music and not be stirred to rhythmic movement of one kind or another. We tap our feet, clap our hands, drum with our fingers, sway our bodies, we hum, sing, whistle. When we carry this innate response to its ultimate expression we find ourselves dancing.

The ability to dance is born in each of us, and the yearning to dance is as much a part of our emotional fiber as hunger, fear, and love. All societies, from the most primitive to the most cultured, share a common need for and appreciation of dancing.

"Dancing," wrote Havelock Ellis, "is the loftiest, the most moving, the most beautiful of the arts, because it is no mere translation or abstraction from life—it is life itself."

Every person is a potential dancer. Some may dance better than others, but all can learn to dance well enough to enjoy it. Many feel the urge to dance but don't know how to express it. Learning to respond to the basic rhythms opens up a delightful new world.

Social dancing today is one of the most popular pastimes in the world. It is enjoyed in every country, by people of all ages. Good dancers are always in demand; they have an asset in making new friends and generally improving their social standing. Dancing is healthfully stimulating, both mentally and physically. The cares and frustrations of the workaday world seem to vanish on the dance floor. Age is no barrier. A recent Mambo competition was won by a youngster of seventy-five, dancing with his twenty-year-old granddaughter!

In this era of push-buttons and automobiles, most of us need to get more exercise. Why not dance? All that you need is a radio or phonograph, a few square yards of floor area, a congenial partner, and a little dancing know-how. Or why not organize a dance party and invite your friends? The more the merrier!

Perhaps the best reason to learn to dance is that it's fun. Most people have a whale of a good time on the dance floor, and there's no reason in the world you can't join them.

CHAPTER THREE

How to Use This Book

IF you can walk, if you can count to four, if you can tell the difference between fast and slow, then you can teach yourself to become a good dancer by following the step-by-step course of instruction in this book. Remember, though, that you will never learn to dance by sitting in an overstuffed chair. Don't just scan the text and diagrams—get up on your feet and do as the words and pictures instruct you to do!

Even if you already know some of the steps, promise yourself that you will start at the beginning of the book and work through to the end, lesson by lesson, pattern by pattern, without skipping ahead. The steps in this book progress in stages, advancing from the simplest patterns to the more complex. Your success with Chapter 17, therefore, will depend on how well you understand Chapters 13 through 16. Take each lesson in its prescribed sequence and you'll find yourself learning faster and better.

When you begin learning a new pattern, be sure to read carefully the printed directions that accompany the step diagram. Then walk through the pattern slowly, without music, until you can do it without referring to the book and without counting aloud or looking down at your feet. Now add the rhythm, as indicated in the diagram by the words "Quick" and "Slow." When you can do it rhythmically, try it to music. Only when you can execute the steps with automatic ease and grace, and in time to music, should you dance a pattern with a partner.

After you have mastered a complete series of steps in this fashion, the final touch to be added is the proper body motion. With the Astaire Fox Trot, for example, you will learn the "side rock." With the Rumba, you will learn the correct hip movement. This extra refinement enhances your technique on the dance floor, adding a graceful line to your body. The subject of styling is treated at the end of each complete dance lesson. Also at the end of each lesson are appropriate combinations of the steps you have just learned.

Before you even look at the initial lesson, make sure you read carefully Section II entitled "The Fundamentals of Good Dancing." Read every word, whether it pertains to the man or the girl, for the better each partner understands the other's role, the better teammate he or she will make on the dance floor.

You may become discouraged about halfway through the lessons. Perhaps you'll find yourself having difficulty doing one of the more intricate steps to the proper musical tempo. Maybe you'll suddenly be unable to remember anything without constantly referring back to the book.

If this happens to you, don't give up or tell yourself that you'll never be a dancer. Many people experience these setbacks in the course of learning. The best antidote is a dose of stick-to-itiveness. And once you've overcome this temporary blackout, it's generally clear sailing right through the remainder of the lessons.

You will undoubtedly find it helpful to watch other people dancing whenever you get the opportunity. Watch the good dancers and see what they are doing that makes them excel. Watch the poor dancers, too, and try to spot their mistakes. Don't worry —you'll soon be able to distinguish the bad from the good dancers!

When you have completed the lessons here, you should be able to do all the most popular dances currently in vogue: Fox Trot, Waltz, Cha Cha Cha, Mambo, Lindy, Rumba, Tango, Samba, Merengue, Polka, Swing Trot, etc. Moreover, you will have learned to dance them in the natural and relaxed style that is so successfully taught at all the Fred Astaire Dance Studios.

Section Two: The Fundamentals of Good Dancing

CHAPTER FOUR

Correct Dancing Posture and Hold

POSTURE

IT is important to perfect good posture early in your dancing career, otherwise you may form bad habits that are difficult to overcome later on. Remember that you dance with your entire body, not only with your feet. How you appear on the dance floor depends largely upon how you hold your head, arms, and torso. When people watch you dance, they look at all of you, from head to toe.

The best way to develop good dancing posture in your home is to practice in front of a full-length mirror, as you would do at a dance studio. You can learn without a mirror, but it helps immensely to be able to see yourself as others see you.

1. The first thing to do is to stand erect. Relax and don't stiffen your spine like a wooden soldier. You should feel comfortable and natural.

2. Hold your head high. Look straight ahead, not at the floor.

3. Chest out and shoulders back. Avoid squaring the shoulders rigidly; you don't have to pass inspection at West Point. Hold yourself tall but with your body relaxed and limber.

4. Now, unlock your knees and flex your legs very slightly. This should give you a feeling of readiness to move without tenseness or stiffness.

5. Raise your heels slightly off the floor, placing your weight evenly on the balls of your feet. If you find it difficult to maintain your balance you've probably lifted your heels a bit too high. Experiment until you can balance easily.

6. In this position, try walking around the room a few times. Pretend that you are dancing. Hum a little melody and tread lightly in time to the rhythm, holding your arms as if you were dancing with someone. Keep your elbows at a comfortable level. Holding them too high is both tiring and old-fashioned; holding them too low will look ungainly.

7. As you move about the room in this fashion, having checked your posture in the mirror, take a look down at your feet. Are you moving them in a straight line? Are you keeping them close together (3 or 4 inches apart)? Nothing will so utterly ruin your appearance on the dance floor as dancing with your feet too far apart. It helps also to point your toes outward slightly and in the direction your foot moves. This should not be exaggerated, however.

Don't stop practicing until you can move around the room in accordance with all the above pointers and feel natural doing it. Practice walking forward and backward, taking long steps and short ones, concentrating on rhythm and grace.

BALLROOM HOLD

When you have learned to hold your body correctly and to move lightly on your feet, you will find it much easier to adopt a comfortable position with a partner. The main thing to keep in mind when dancing with someone is that height largely determines the type of hold used. When both partners are approximately the same height, or when the girl is slightly shorter than her partner, the normal Ballroom Hold is used. This hold is used for the three Progressive Dances—the Fox Trot, Waltz, and Tango. Study the points listed below carefully before attempting to assume the Ballroom Hold with a partner, and remember your correct posture.

1. Stand erect and with your feet together.

2. Both partners raise their arms slightly, so that the elbows are held away from the body.

3. The man places his right hand lightly but firmly against the small of the girl's back, slightly to the left side.

4. The man holds his partner parallel and slightly to the right of him. This is the most natural position, and the majority of dancers assume it automatically, even as beginning students.

5. The man holds his left hand in an upward direction with the palm facing his partner. He should relax his hand and not clench his fist.

6. The girl places her right hand between the man's left thumb and forefinger, making sure not to clutch the man's hand.

7. The girl places her left hand slightly behind the man's right shoulder, with her thumb resting on top of his shoulder. Her left arm should rest lightly on the man's right arm.

8. In the normal Ballroom Hold, both partners should stand close enough together so that body contact is made. This is important in the Progressive Dances as body contact facilitates the man's lead.

When a tall man is dancing with a short girl, body contact is eliminated. The man should adjust the position of his right hand so that it is slightly below the girl's left shoulder blade. The girl should adjust the position of her left hand, placing it comfortably to the side of the man's right shoulder.

The hold assumed for the Rhythm Dances—the Mambo, Rumba, Cha Cha Cha, etc. (the remainder of the dances in this book)—is basically the same as the Ballroom Hold. The main difference is that body contact is not necessary, because these dances are generally limited to a smaller area on the dance floor and do not progress around the room in the same manner as the Fox Trot, Waltz, and Tango.

The student who has mastered the rules of good posture and a good Ballroom Hold will enjoy a head start in learning the skills that eventually qualify him as a desirable, popular dancing partner.

CHAPTER FIVE
Keeping Time to the Music

ANYONE who can hum, whistle, sing a melody, or move some part of his body in time to music can become an accomplished ballroom dancer. A great deal of musical ability is not prerequisite to good dancing. Even if your "Mary Had a Little Lamb" sounds like "God Save the Queen" you can go right ahead and learn to dance as well as the next person. For you can easily train yourself to keep time to music, and at the same time cultivate your sense of rhythm.

Sit down, relax, and just listen to some dance music for a few minutes—a slow ballad, a swing tune, a Latin American number, it doesn't matter what. Feel the underlying beat of the music? Doesn't it arouse a regular rhythmic pulse in you, make you want to tap your foot or drum your fingers?

Usually the timing is accented by the drum or bass fiddle so you'll have no trouble picking up the beat. For example, if you were listening to the music of "Some Enchanted Evening," you would feel an unmistakable beat on the word "Some," on the second syllable of the word "Enchanted," and on both syllables of the word "Evening:"

Some En - *chan* - ted *Eve* - *ning*
beat 1 beat 2 beat 3 beat 4

Those four accents, or pulses that you feel from the music to those three words, are the beats that you will follow when you dance.* That's really all there is to keeping time when you dance. You listen for the regular beat of the music and let it govern how fast or slow you step around the dance floor.

Even if you can't tell one melody from another you will still be able to pick up the beat of the music from the rhythm section of the band. As a matter of fact, you should not confuse the melody with the rhythm. For example, "White Christmas" and "Smoke Gets in Your Eyes" each have their own distinctive melody. But both were written to be played in the same time—4 beats to a measure. Therefore you would dance a Fox Trot in precisely the same manner whether the band played the one song or the other.

When you begin working with the step diagrams later in this book and start counting the patterns, you will see the terms "Slow" and "Quick." It is important that you know the following simple rules about the timing of these steps:

Any step labeled "Slow" is given two beats of music.

Any step labeled "Quick" is given one beat of music.

For example, if you were dancing to the music of "Some Enchanted Evening" and doing the Basic Astaire One Step shown on page 35, this is how you would apply the Slow, Quick, Quick rhythm to the step diagram:

The beats of the music would fall as follows:

Some	en - *chan*-ted	*eve*	*ning*	. . . . .	. . . . .	. . . . .	**
beat 1	beat 2	beat 3	beat 4	beat 1	beat 2	beat 3	beat 4
You may	*see* a	*stran* -	*ger*	. . . . .	. . . . .	. . . . .	**
beat 1	beat 2	beat 3	beat 4	beat 1	beat 2	beat 3	beat 4

You would take the first step with your left foot, touching it to the floor on the word "Some." Since that first step is Slow you would hold it in place for two beats. On the third beat (which falls on the first syllable of "evening") you would touch the floor with your right foot, completing the first two steps. Since the second step is marked Quick, the third step would be taken on the very next beat: you would close with your left foot on the second syllable of "evening," thereby completing the first three steps of the six that make up the One Step. The next three steps follow in the same sequence beginning with the beat right after the last syllable of "evening." The rhythm of the entire six-step sequence of the One Step, showing how it is repeated, may be indicated as follows:

*When just before beginning a song the orchestra leader looks at his men and says "Four beats to the bar," he is telling them that the song is in basic 4/4 timing. This means that the beats will fall into groups of four, the main accent coming on the first beat of each group—as in the case of "Some Enchanted Evening." Each group of four beats makes up one measure, or bar, of the song. Since so many popular songs are written that way, one often hears the phrase "Four beats to the bar." (A waltz has three beats to the bar, the main accent falling on the first beat.)

**Even though the melody pauses—remains suspended, so to speak—after the words "evening" and "stranger," the beats continue at the regular rate of rhythm established by the orchestra. Therefore, the steps of the dance will move right along in time with the beats—not with the lyrics or the particular melody being played.

Some en -	*chan* ted	*eve* -	*ning*	. . . . . .			
beat 1	beat 2	beat 3	beat 4	beat 1	beat 2	beat 3	beat 4
1st step		2nd step	3rd step	4th step		5th step	6th step
S — l — o — w		Quick	Quick	S — l — o — w		Quick	Quick

You may	*see* a	*stran* -	*ger*	. . . . . .			
beat 1	beat 2	beat 3	beat 4	beat 1	beat 2	beat 3	beat 4
1st step		2nd step	3rd step	4th step		5th step	6th step
S — l — o — w		Quick	Quick	S — l — o — w		Quick	Quick

If there is *no* "Slow" or "Quick" indicated, each step is taken in strict time to the music—one step to one beat.

If the word "And" appears in the diagram, it represents a step to be danced twice as fast as the normal count, or two steps to the beat. In the Polka, for instance, there is a tiny half-beat hop taken at the beginning of a pattern. You count "And, Quick, Quick, Slow," therefore you take a half-beat step, a one-beat step, another one-beat step, and two-beat step.

If a step precedes a half-beat step, it too becomes a half-beat step. For example, in a sequence marked "Quick And Quick," the first two steps receive a half beat apiece, and the last step one beat.

All this may sound very complicated to you at present, but you should have no difficulty if you stand up right now, count four beats aloud, and just *walk* in time to your cadence count: One, Two, Three, Four. First, take one step to each beat. This amounts to simple marching, but in terms of dancing you are taking Quick steps—one to each beat. Next, take one step to every two beats. These would be Slow steps. If you do them correctly you will be taking two Slow steps to every four beats. After this, try doing a sequence of Slow, Quick, Quick steps: begin with your left foot on the count of one, hold it in place on the count of two, then a step with your right foot on three followed by another with your left on four, and start the sequence again with your right on the count of one. Finally, try several sequences of Quick And Quick. In doing this, take a step with your left following it immediately by a step with your right so that you will be ready for the third step (with your left foot) on the count of two. Do the same on counts three and four (this time starting with the right foot) as you have done on counts one and two, thereby repeating the sequence. When you think you've caught on, try all these steps to slow music, assuming the correct dancing posture. As your proficiency increases, try them to fast music.

These are all the step tempos you need to know in social dancing. If you move according to directions in the diagrams, you will automatically add the right rhythm to the pattern you are learning.

If you can read music—and if you can't, don't let it worry you—it will help you to know that all the dances in this book, except the Waltz and the Polka, are counted with four beats to the bar. The Waltz is always counted with three beats to the bar; the Polka, with two beats to each bar.

CHAPTER SIX

On the Dance Floor

THE best time to learn how to progress properly around a dance floor is while you are practicing the step patterns alone in your home. By doing this, you will accustom yourself to moving automatically in the right direction, thus avoiding difficulty later on. Nobody, after all, is going to be popular if he is forever bucking traffic on the dance floor, causing jams and collisions.

Since almost all dance floors are rectangular or square, it makes sense to travel such a course around the room. However, you don't have to make abrupt ninety-degree turns at the corner. Simply dance along an oval route. It really doesn't matter as long as you follow the general flow of traffic.

It is the custom to travel around the dance floor in a counterclockwise direction. For the man this means that if you walk around the perimeter of a dance floor, the center is to your left. As you get on the floor, you should start dancing toward the wall on your right. Although when you dance you take frequent steps backward or to the side, your over-all direction should be counterclockwise. Since the man is the leader, direction is his responsibility. When he wishes to execute a back or side step, he should first make certain that the maneuver will not interfere with another couple's progress.

As you'll see when you actually try it on the dance floor, it's merely a matter of taking the course of least resistance, of being considerate of other people's right of way.

CHAPTER SEVEN

Being A Good Leader

ON the dance floor, the man is the boss. He must set the pace for his partner, navigate a proper course around the dance floor, choose the step patterns, and dance in time with the music. At the same time, he is expected to indicate to his partner where he is heading and what he wants to do.

Obviously, then, to be a good leader, you must first of all be able to dance; that is, you must develop a working knowledge of the steps and patterns. Knowing the steps, however, is only half the responsibility. You must also be able to communicate your intentions to the girl quickly, subtly, and meaningfully.

How do you do this? With your body, right arm and hand. Always place your right hand against the small of your partner's back. If this is too far to reach comfortably, move your hand a little to the side, but not up or down. Keep it just above her waist. As you dance she will respond naturally to a gentle pressure of your hand. A slight nudge to the right, and she will follow you in that direction. A slight pull toward you as you step back, and she will move forward.

Never try to lead with your left hand. You will be stiffening your elbow in order to push your arm against your partner's. Her normal reaction will be to push right back and before you know it you will look like a pair of Indian wrestlers. Always keep your left hand in line with your left shoulder; raise it only when you lead an underarm turn.

When dancing with a girl for the first time, it is a good idea to begin with the basic steps and progress in stages toward the more intricate steps. In this way you will have an opportunity to get better acquainted with one another's technique and limitations. Of course the more often you dance with a particular partner, the better will be the rapport between you. It's when you take a new partner out on the dance floor that you must exert the most skill in leading.

Among the worst offenses you can commit is to force your partner to exceed her ability. Instead of impressing her as a superior dancer, you'll only convince her that you need a few lessons in common courtesy. Nobody likes a show-off, particularly when he is showing off at another person's expense.

Try to make the dance as pleasant as possible for your partner. Aside from being gallant, try to enhance a girl's appearance on the floor. Certainly the best way to accomplish this is to dance well.

Even if you've danced with a girl a thousand times, don't be ashamed at the beginning of each dance to pause a moment, listen to the music, and check the tempo. Rushing right into a Rumba can make you look pretty foolish if the band is playing a Cha Cha Cha.

But what if you are halfway through the dance and suddenly discover you're not in step to the music? Well, don't panic—it happens to the finest of dancers. The obvious remedy is to pick up the proper tempo again as quickly and gracefully as possible. Rather than attempt a drastic adjustment in the middle of a pattern, however, you should finish the step sequence, pause, and start over. The trick is to glide to a gradual stop, in a foot position that is convenient and natural, and mark time for a few beats before stepping off again.

The ultimate measure of your expertness as a leader is the grace and flowing line of your dancing. Avoid making sudden, jerky shifts in your step patterns; each pattern should merge smoothly and fluidly into the next. Make a habit of leading a step at least two or three times in succession before beginning a new pattern. By not switching patterns too frequently, you avoid frenetic, disjointed sequences. Also, you give yourself time to plan ahead, which reduces the likelihood of your stumbling hurriedly into an inappropriate pattern. Keep in mind that, above all, dancing is an expression of artful motion.

A few final words of advice: Don't count time aloud, either for your own or your partner's edification. And never explain to her in words what you want her to do next. Both of these blunders are confessions of incompetence as a leader. If you know your own part well, perform it with practiced confidence, and lead with your body and your right hand, you'll find you are doing all that is necessary to win approval as captain of the team.

Ten Rules a Man Should Review

1. When you dance, keep your body relaxed, with your weight held over the soles of your shoes, heels **slightly** off the floor. Point toes slightly outward. Stand erect, but not rigid.

2. Move in time to the beat, not the melody, of the music.

3. In order to be a good leader, do only those dance patterns you know well enough to do gracefully to the music and without thinking about your footwork.

4. Travel around the dance floor in a counterclockwise direction. When stepping forward, your right arm should be closest to the wall most of the time.

5. Always begin dancing on your left foot. There are no exceptions to this rule.

6. Hold your partner in front and slightly to the right of you. Look over her right shoulder to see where you are going. Lead with your entire body and your right hand, holding it against the small of your partner's back and a little to the side. Lift your elbows away from your body, keeping your left hand in line with your shoulder.

7. It is wiser to pause in position at the beginning of a new dance and check your timing than to start off in the wrong tempo.

8. Avoid awkward shifts in your pattern sequences by leading the same step at least two or three times in succession. Plan ahead and strive for smooth transitions.

9. **Never** count aloud, look down at your feet, or tell your companion verbally what steps you want to do next.

10. Practice makes perfect.

CHAPTER EIGHT

Being A Good Follower

THE major qualification for being a good follower is that you know your part well, at least as well as the man knows his. In fact, the popular girl as a rule knows the dance patterns so well that she could lead if called upon to do so.

When you start working with the step diagrams in this book, memorize the count and the pattern by walking through it a few times. Be sure to read carefully the printed instructions accompanying each diagram, and study all the drawings on the page. When you've learned all the steps of a dance, add the proper body motion. Only when you can do a step by memory, without constantly checking back to the book or counting aloud or staring down at your footwork, should you try it to music—slowly at first, then fast. And only when you can do it effortlessly to music should you try it with a partner. A feeling of self-assurance is usually a good indication of your ability. As you become interested in the steps and experience the pleasant sensation of moving in rhythm, you'll find yourself enjoying the lessons, anticipating every new challenge. And soon you'll realize that dancing really isn't difficult at all.

It is wise to study the man's part before you begin learning your own. By visualizing your partner's movements and analyzing them, you will obtain a better mental picture of your role in the partnership.

Note that in most patterns your part is the exact opposite of the man's part. When he starts by walking forward with his left foot, you move backward with your right. Since forward steps feel more natural than backward steps, the man's part will be easier to execute than the girl's part. By walking through his pattern a few times, you're likely to have less touble with your own.

It is extremely important for you to develop a long, graceful backward step. Most girls make the mistake of taking such small backward steps that their feet are constantly being stepped on by their partners. When stepping backward, they either place the sole of their shoe on the floor or attempt to place their foot down flat immediately, causing the step to become shorter than it should be.

Practice the points listed below slowly, until the movement becomes natural to you:

1. Start with your feet together.

2. Stretch your right leg backward so that only the tip of the toe touches the floor. Keep your body weight on your left foot until the next movement.

3. Now let your weight begin to transfer onto the right foot. Slowly let the weight go onto the sole, then lower the heel so that the entire foot touches the floor.

4. As the entire right foot touches the floor, release all weight from the left foot, and slowly begin to draw it up to the right foot. (Without stopping, you will draw your left foot slowly past your right in beginning to execute step No. 5.)

5. Now do the same backward movement with the left foot, stretching the tip of the toe first, then slowly putting your weight onto the sole, and finally with foot flat.

If you find yourself losing your balance, you are probably letting your body weight shift too soon. Remember, when the tip of your toe is touching the floor, your body weight is not yet transferred. You begin to transfer when you begin lowering the sole of your foot.

Practice this backward movement several times until it feels natural and relaxed. When you have perfected the movement, you will look light on your feet and you'll feel that way!

Once you develop a graceful, long backward movement, your feet will not be stepped on by your partner; furthermore you will strengthen your muscles and sharpen your sense of balance. You should also be able to dance with virtually any partner, tall or short, regardless of whether he takes large or small strides.

To attain good balance when dancing with a partner and better to follow his lead, remember the rules for correct posture and the dance position Hold explained earlier in this book. Practice dancing in partnership position when you are alone in order to train your arm muscles. Last, but not least, concede right now that the man is in command on the dance floor. No matter how unfavorably you regard your partner's dancing ability, *never* try to wrest the lead away from him. If you do not enjoy dancing with him, just refuse his next invitation.

Ten Rules a Girl Should Review

1. Don't labor under the delusion that it is the man who must know how to dance while the girl has only to follow along as best she can. To be a popular partner, you must know the steps and be as accomplished a dancer as the man.

2. Feel confidence in yourself by knowing the dance patterns and styling of many dances.

3. By understanding the man's part, you'll find it simpler to learn yours. The best girl dancers are capable of leading if called upon to do so.

4. The man is the leader on the dance floor. Follow his lead at all times. Be ready to move lightly to each step he takes and, above all, don't tell him what or how to dance while on the dance floor.

5. Don't hinder your partner's freedom of motion. Develop a long, graceful backward step. The shorter steps will then come naturally and you'll be able to adjust easily to your partner's stride.

6. Always begin dancing on your right foot. In most cases, your first step will be backwards, though there are exceptions.

7. Place your left hand slightly behind your partner's right shoulder. Let your thumb rest upon his shoulder to achieve good balance and to follow his lead with extra precision. Don't lean or hang on your partner. Remain light on your feet.

8. Never count aloud or glance down at your feet while dancing. This shows a definite lack of self-confidence.

9. Always be polite and pleasant. If you are a congenial companion your partner will forgive a few shortcomings in your dancing.

10. Practice makes perfect.

CHAPTER NINE

Remember Your Manners

GOOD manners are just as fundamental to successful dancing as is correct footwork. And good dancing never compensates for poor manners. It's not corny or old-fashioned to be courteous; it's just common sense if you expect to have fun and meet people at a dance. Being courteous does not mean that you have to be excessively formal or a martinet about the social niceties. Etiquette, after all, consists of nothing more than a respect for the feelings of others.

When you accept an invitation to a dance party, you tacitly agree to satisfy certain obligations. You are expected to be well-groomed and suitably attired, in an amiable mood, and able to dance. In addition, you are expected to live up to the special rules of etiquette that help promote a good time for everyone at a dance.

To begin with, the man should ask the girl to dance in a simple and direct way. "May I have the next dance?" or "Will you dance with me?" are two satisfactory approaches.

A man should contribute to the convivial atmosphere of the party by mingling with the group and changing partners. Girls, too, should not monopolize their favorite partners. If a couple wants to dance every dance together, they can always go to a public ballroom or to a supper club or turn on the phonograph at home. Parties are made for meeting and mixing with people, especially dance parties.

A man should make every effort to dance with his hostess. Likewise, unless she has a very good reason, a girl should not refuse to dance with her host.

It is not good form for a girl to suggest to a man that they dance together, the only exceptions being when he is a member of her family or a very close friend. Her own sense of propriety should be her guide. Also, a girl should be careful not to insult a would-be partner by the way she refuses his invitation. If she wants to decline, she should be diplomatic and offer a plausible excuse. At the same time, she ought not to dance with a man if she really dislikes him and can't hide her feelings.

When a girl does accept a man's invitation, she quite properly expects to be escorted to the dance floor and, afterwards, back to where she was sitting. The rudest thing a man can do is to leave his partner standing in the middle of the room at the end of a dance. And he should remember to thank her for being his partner even if he's straining the truth. If the partnership was a flop, he doesn't have to dance with her again.

Many men are not quite sure about cutting in on a girl while a dance is in progress. In the United States, this is an accepted custom. In foreign countries, it may or may not be condoned; it is advisable to inquire about the practice before finding you've committed a *faux pas*. If you attend a dance in the United States where cutting in is not allowed, you'll probably be told this when the festivities begin.

How should a man go about cutting in? He should wait until the girl is dancing near one side of the dance floor, not barge out into the center, getting in everyone's way. Then he can easily go over and say to her partner: "May I cut in?" or "Do you mind if I cut in?"

For the man who is dancing to refuse or show any sign of displeasure is poor behavior. The same holds true for the girl. She should not exhibit disappointment, neither should she lunge for her new partner with great glee.

Is it permissible for the original partner to wait for a few minutes and then cut right back in? Not unless there has been an intervening cut-in. For example, if Tom cuts in on Harry, Harry may not do the same to Tom. He should wait until another man is dancing with the girl or until Tom starts the following dance with the same girl. Were it not for this rule, Tom and Harry might be cutting in on each other so often that there would be no time left for dancing.

At a private dance party, unless a rule has been made to the contrary, a man is at liberty to cut in on any couple. Since everyone is an invited guest, all are presumed to know one another or to have been introduced. At a public dance, however, or in a restaurant or night club, a man should not try to cut in on strangers, nor should he permit a stranger to cut in on his partner.

Among the worst offenders of dance etiquette are the following:

The Show-Off. This bothersome person cannot help demonstrating his dancing prowess, to the great annoyance of everybody in the vicinity. He shows no consideration for his partner or anyone else within kicking and bumping range. The show-off is a floor hog. Whether leader or follower, this character drags his partner around the room in a state of mingled terror, embarrassment, and rage.

Wrong-Way Charlie. Although everyone else on the dance floor has enough sense to follow the counterclockwise flow of traffic, Charlie plows upstream as though he and his cowering partner were bucking the line in the Rose Bowl.

The Chatterbox. The chatterbox is a constant source of irritation on a dance floor. Unfortunately, there are always a few at every dance. They prattle incessantly into their partners' ears, usually about the most boring topics. When they're at their worst, the constant babble is so voluminous that it drowns out the music.

The Iceberg. Meet the stern, silent, stone-faced male and the frosty, forbidding female. Neither utters a syllable. Their lips are frozen in a grim, thin line. Actually they may be very nice people, but they look so dismal that others avoid them. You don't have to talk while you dance, but at least wear a smile and look as though you're enjoying yourself.

The Tutor. First cousin to the show-off, this unpopular denizen of the dance floor has the unnerving habit of breaking off in the middle of a dance to show you what you're doing wrong. Right in front of everybody you'll get an impromptu lesson. Watch out if he or she asks if you know a certain step. If you answer negatively, you will be taught whether you like it or not.

The Crooner. As the name implies, this nuisance feels called upon to serenade you as you dance. The words to the song may not be intelligible, the tune may be mangled beyond recognition, but there's no stopping this would-be Sinatra's singing.

Or it may be humming. Or whistling. At any rate, if you can't avoid the creature, get a pair of ear stopples.

The Great Lover. This hopeful Don Juan fancies himself an irresistible gift to all womanhood and tries to sweep his partners off their feet with his charm and manliness. His ego is as big as a helium balloon and is just as easily punctured.

The Debator. The debator likes to sound off on politics, religion, or maybe it's child psychology. He invariably brings up subjects likely to arouse strong partisan feelings. He loves to argue. But the dance floor is not a debating arena. If you must pit your point of view against your companion's, leave the floor or continue the discussion at another time.

The Quitter. This individual is always eager to start a dance, but never lasts until the end. There is nothing wrong with asking a partner to sit out the remainder of a dance with you, but you should never imply that your partner's dancing is unsatisfactory. The trouble with the quitter is that he wants to sit down in the middle of every dance and doesn't bother with explanations. It's "Let dance!" or "I'd love to dance!" and then, a few seconds later, "Let's sit down!"

The Jolly Extrovert. It's almost impossible to miss the jolly extrovert on the dance floor. While dancing, he completely ignores his partner in order to talk with another couple or someone along the sidelines. Typically, he shouts his greetings across the entire room.

CHAPTER TEN

The Dance Positions

UNTIL now, in our discussions of ballroom dancing, we have described the position you will be using most of the time, that is, the basic ballroom position or the *closed position.* (See drawing above.) In addition, however, there are six other positions that every social dancer should know. Each of these positions will be employed in one or more of the step patterns you study in this book. Simply read about them now and study the accompanying drawings; or perhaps you will find it easier to practice them now with an imaginary partner.

1. Right Side Position. This is actually a variation of the closed position. The man simply moves to the girl's right and continues executing the patterns as in the closed position. The partners do not let go of one another or change the direction in which they are facing. However, instead of the man putting his left foot to the floor between the girl's feet, as in the closed position, he dances with both of his feet to the right of her right foot. She, too, is dancing with both her feet to the right of her partner's. In other words, the man and the girl are dancing right side to right side, facing each other, one moving forward as the other moves back.

2. Left Side Position. This is done exactly as the above position, except that the man moves to the girl's left. His feet are both to the left of her left foot; her feet are both to the left of his left foot. Again, the partners face each other as they dance left side to left side. Nor do they let go of each other or change their hand positions.

3. Right Open Position. (This is also called the **counter promenade position.)** Dancing from the closed position, the partners separate slightly in order to face the same direction. The man simply turns the right side of his body slightly away from the girl. The girl turns the left side of her body slightly away from the man. Thus the man is dancing to the right of the girl, facing in the same direction. The hands may be held the same as in the closed position, or the man may release his right hand hold.

4. Left Open Position. This is also called the **conversation** or **promenade position.** Same as above, except that the man dances on the girl's left side, both of them facing in the same direction.

To accomplish this position from the **closed position,** the man turns the left side of his body slightly away from the girl; the girl turns the right side of her body slightly away from the man. The man's hand remains on the girl's waist. The girl's left hand stays upon his shoulder.

To accomplish this position from **right open position,** the man and girl will both turn their bodies as previously described. However, the man will hold the girl's left hand in his right hand, rather than placing his right hand on the girl's waist. The man will also release his left hand hold, so that contact is maintained solely with the man's right hand and the girl's left hand.

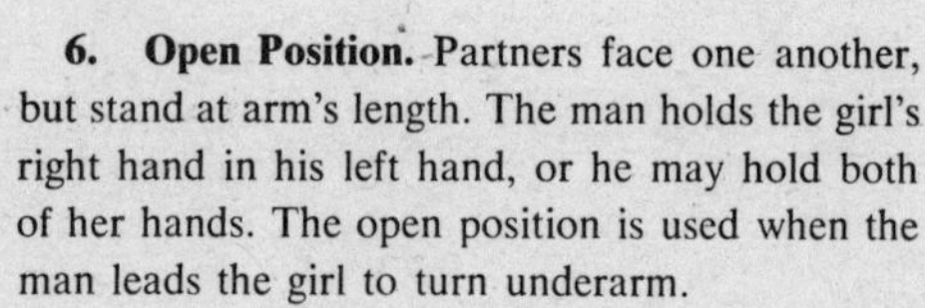

5. Apart Position. Partners are separated, standing approximately at arm's length, with no physical contact between them. They may, at the leader's discretion, dance on identical feet or on opposite feet.

6. Open Position. Partners face one another, but stand at arm's length. The man holds the girl's right hand in his left hand, or he may hold both of her hands. The open position is used when the man leads the girl to turn underarm.

CHAPTER ELEVEN

Follow-Through

THE value of follow-through to the dancer cannot be overestimated. It represents the graceful execution of a motion from start to finish; it provides control and balance, enabling the dancer to move fluidly, blending each movement into the next. Follow-through is especially important for the inexperienced dancer whose balance and timing are not yet fully developed. For expert dancers, follow-through is second nature, and this is one reason they move so gracefully. As a beginner, you should always be conscious of your follow-through, endeavoring to perfect it, never forgetting to practice it.

Though follow-through is an essential ingredient in your over-all movement, it is particularly important in your footwork, in the way you advance your feet from one floor position to the next. Suppose you have just taken a forward step with your left foot and now have to move your right foot. How can you make the step as graceful and light as possible? You don't merely pick it up, swing it forward, and put it down again. This would be tantamount to plain, simple walking.

Begin by taking a step forward with your left foot. As you bring your right foot forward, pass it close by the inside of your supporting left foot. Now take another step forward, passing your left foot close by the inside of your right foot. Try to pass your feet as close to each other as you can without having them actually touch. When you are moving forward, remember that the sole of your shoe is the first part of the foot to touch the floor. Don't lift your feet more than an inch or so from the floor. Continue on across the room in this fashion. Turn on the phonograph and do it in time to the music. Surprised at how light you feel on your feet?

No matter which dance you are doing, you should always pass your feet in this fashion as you move forward. This type of follow-through on a forward step is called the *straight follow-through*. If you want to take a step backward, you merely apply the same principles of moving forward to a backward movement.

When you want to take a step to the side, after moving forward or backward, you should use either the straight follow-through or one of the other two styles of follow-through, depending on what dance you are doing. The following diagrams show only the man's part since the follow-through is the same for girls.

Note: In the following dance step diagrams

All Right feet are shaded **All** Left feet are unshaded

GIRL MAN GIRL MAN

Fox Trot. When you want to take a step to the side after moving forward or backward, use the straight follow-through. (See diagram.)

STRAIGHT FOLLOW-THROUGH (applied to the Fox Trot One Step—Man's Part: Forward—dotted line indicates follow-through)

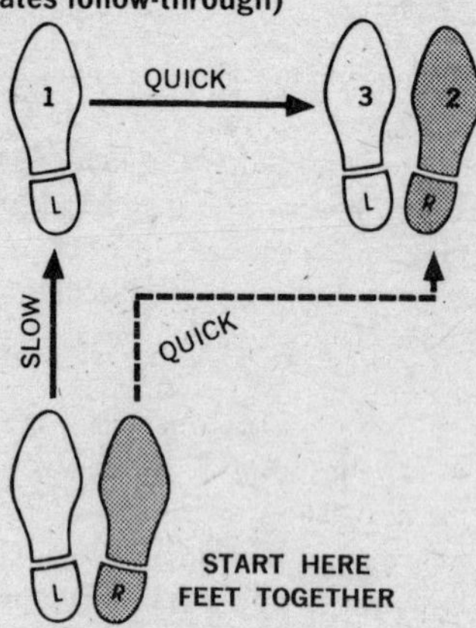

Waltz, Mambo, Samba. When you want to take a step to the side, after moving forward or backward, use the *curved follow-through.* Instead of passing the moving foot close by the inside of the supporting foot, pass it along a slight outwardly curving line. (See diagram.)

CURVED FOLLOW-THROUGH (applied to the Waltz Progressive Basic Step—Man's Part: Forward—dotted line indicates follow-through)

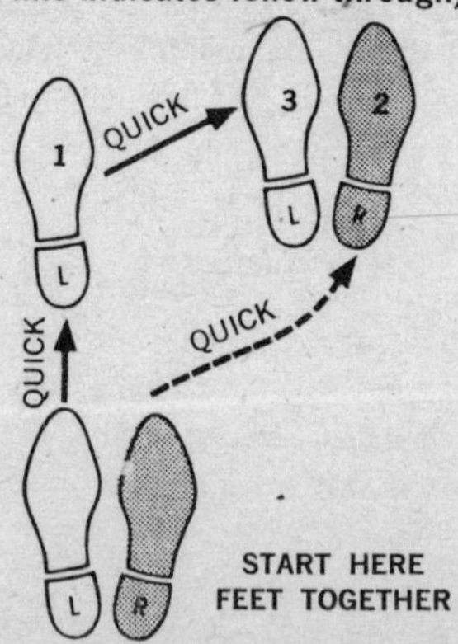

Tango, Rumba, Cha Cha Cha, Merengue. When you want to take a step to the side, after moving forward or backward, use the *angular follow-through.* Here the moving foot travels along a direct line to the side, rather than a curved line. The angular follow-through resembles the hypotenuse of a triangle. (See diagram.)

You should learn the three styles of follow-through and the corresponding dances for which they are used. Study the accompanying drawings and practice your follow-through, remembering that your objective is to have each movement flow right into the next.

ANGULAR FOLLOW-THROUGH (applied to the Tango Basic Closed Step—Man's Part: Forward—dotted line indicates follow-through)

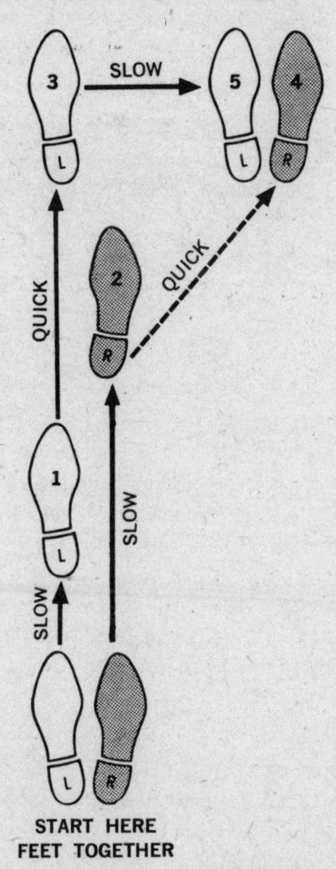

CHAPTER TWELVE

Contrabody Movement

A good dancer accomplishes graceful turns—whether they be quarter turns, half turns, full turns, double turns, or triple turns—by the proper use of *contrabody movement*. If you watch a good dancer closely, you'll see that as he takes a step with his right foot, he swings the left side of his body towards that foot, and vice versa. This action of turning the opposite hip and shoulder toward the moving leg facilitates the art of rotation. It is of particular value to the dancer in the start of all turning figures. Since there are four ways of turning in dancing, there are four ways in which contrabody movement can be executed:

1. **Forward Turn to Right.** Step forward with the right foot and at the same time swing the left hip and shoulder forward.

2. **Forward Turn to Left.** Step forward with the left foot and simultaneously swing the right hip and shoulder forward.

3. **Backward Turn to Right.** Step back with the left foot and at the same time swing the right hip and shoulder backward.

4. **Backward Turn to Left.** Step back with the right foot and simultaneously swing the left hip and shoulder backward.

This contrary swing of the body is a fluid motion which is timed to coincide with your footwork. Do not twist your body, or jerk it suddenly forward or back; make it a relaxed accompaniment to the step, a slight leaning into the turn. Until you actually begin working with the step diagrams, practice this contrabody movement slowly and carefully.

Section Three: The Lessons

CHAPTER THIRTEEN
Before You Start The Lessons

PRIOR to walking through any step diagram, carefully study the printed instructions and the accompanying drawings. In some of the more complicated patterns, the girl may find it easier to visualize her part if she first walks through the man's part two or three times.

To teach yourself to dance the Fred Astaire way most efficiently, follow these instructions:

1. Start Here—Feet Together. This sign tells you where the step begins on each diagram. Stand with your feet together. You will then be ready to walk though the pattern.

2. Follow the Numerals. The first step you take is numbered 1; the second step, 2; the third, 3; and so forth. The man always starts dancing with his left foot, the girl with her right foot. In steps where only the heel or toe touches the floor, only that portion of the foot is drawn in the diagram. When a foot is drawn in a broken line, no weight is placed on that foot.

3. Walk Through the Step. Always walk through the step and familiarize yourself with its movements before attempting to do it with proper rhythm and styling.

4. Add the Rhythm. When you have learned the sequence of steps, put the rhythm into the pattern. The rhythm is explained in the diagram by the words "Slow" and "Quick." Review Chapter 5, "Keeping Time to the Music."

5. Make Your Footwork Precise. After you have learned a step sequence to the proper rhythm, walk through it again, trying to keep your footwork neat, clean, and graceful, using follow-through.

6. Add the Proper Body Motion. Developing good body motion takes practice. Much of it will come to you instinctively, and much can be learned by watching other people dance. The best body motion looks relaxed and natural, as though inspired by the music, as indeed it should be. The body motion you should add to each dance is described at the end of each lesson.

You are now ready for the Astaire Fox Trot and a whole new world of dancing fun! Good luck!

CHAPTER FOURTEEN

The Fox Trot

INTRODUCTION

THE Fox Trot is by far the most popular of ballroom dances. Adapted around 1912 from the stage routines of the famed vaudeville dancer Harry Fox, this was the first dance that permitted partners to hold each other closer than arm's length. Since about 1920, the Fox Trot has emphasized individual freedom of dance expression. Perhaps this is why in the past four decades well over seventy-five per cent of all popular songs have been written in Fox Trot tempo.

As styled by Fred Astaire, the Fox Trot is a joyful, creative dance. Simplicity is the guiding principle of styling; every step is keyed to the accent and normal tempo of the music.

Three important considerations to remember while you are dancing the Fox Trot are *direction, follow-through,* and *dance position.* The lessons in this book are designed to help you achieve all three to the best advantage. Make all your forward and backward steps the same size. The length of your stride will depend upon your height and body conformation. A practical rule of thumb is to make your stride as long as you can without losing graceful command of your balance. In general, this stride will be a slight exaggeration of your normal walking stride.

Blend your movements smoothly, with continuity. When you change direction, follow through with your leg and body. Remember the principle of contrabody movement for turning steps. Use every part of your body as you dance, letting the music inspire your movements.

The Fox Trot is a logical starting place for learning to dance. It will teach you basic forward, backward, and side steps that you will later use in other dances. As you progress, you'll see that the Fox Trot, with its fascinating rhythm pattern, affords many opportunities for personal interpretation.

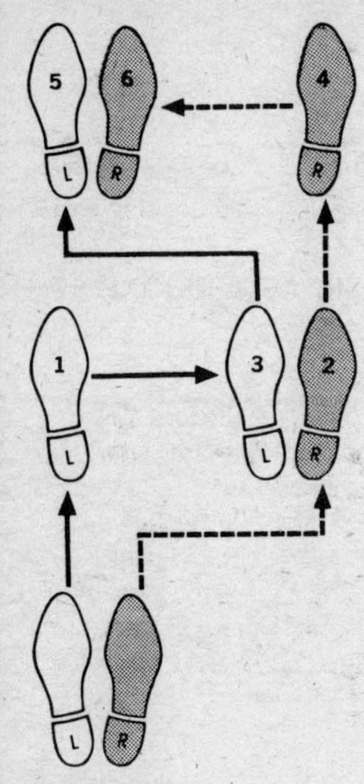

START HERE
FEET TOGETHER

BASIC ASTAIRE ONE STEP

Rhythm: Slow, Quick, Quick
Slow, Quick, Quick

MAN'S PART: Forward

1. Left foot forward, Slow
2. Right foot forward and to side, Quick (use straight follow-through)*
3. Close with left foot, Quick
4. Right foot forward, Slow
5. Left foot forward and to side, Quick (use straight follow-through)
6. Close with right foot, Quick

START HERE
FEET TOGETHER

MAN'S PART: Backward

1. Left foot backward, Slow
2. Right foot backward and to side, Quick (use straight follow-through)
3. Close with left foot, Quick
4. Right foot backward, Slow
5. Left foot backward and to side, Quick (use straight follow-through)
6. Close with right foot, Quick

NOTE: This step is danced in the closed position.

*If necessary, review Chapter 11, "Follow-Through."

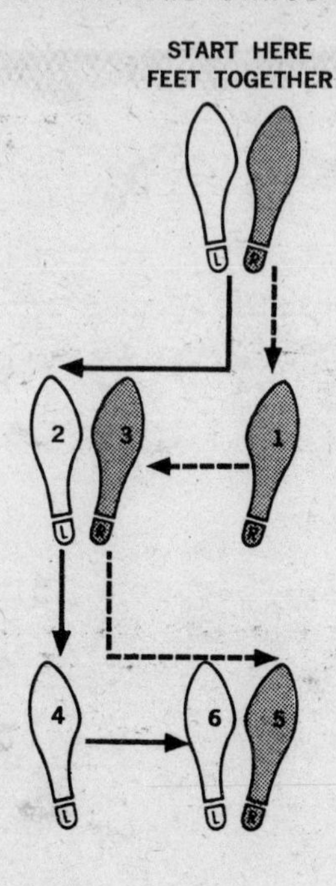

BASIC ASTAIRE ONE STEP

Rhythm: Slow, Quick, Quick
Slow, Quick, Quick

GIRL'S PART: Backward

1. Right foot backward, Slow
2. Left foot backward and to side, Quick (use straight follow-through)*
3. Close with right foot, Quick
4. Left foot backward, Slow
5. Right foot backward and to side, Quick (use straight follow-through)
6. Close with left foot, Quick

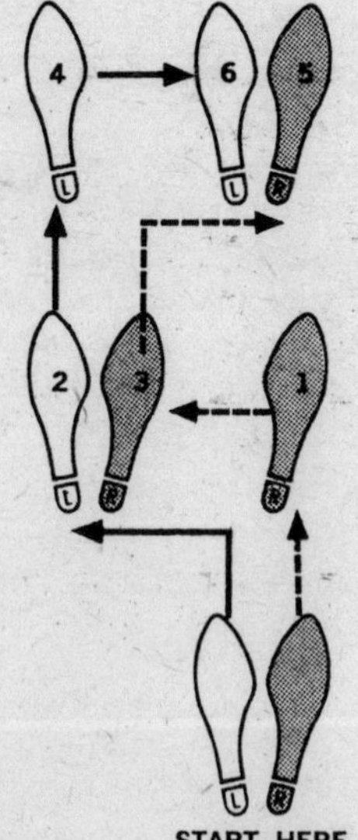

GIRL'S PART: Forward

1. Right foot forward, Slow
2. Left foot forward and to side, Quick (use straight follow-through)
3. Close with right foot, Quick
4. Left foot forward, Slow
5. Right foot forward and to side, Quick (use straight follow-through)
6. Close with left foot, Quick

NOTE: See note under man's part.

*If necessary, review Chapter 11, "Follow-Through."

BASIC ASTAIRE TWO STEP

Rhythm: Slow, Slow, Quick, Quick

GIRL'S PART: Backward

1. Right foot backward, Slow
2. Left foot backward, Slow (use straight follow-through)
3. Right foot backward and to side, Quick (use straight follow-through)
4. Close with left foot, Quick

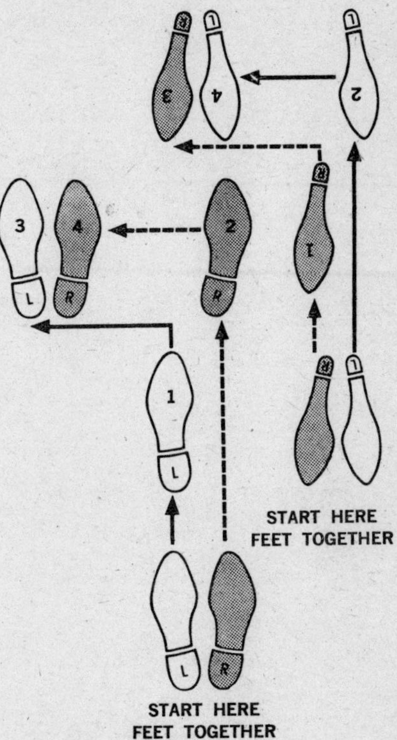

BASIC ASTAIRE TWO STEP

Rhythm: Slow, Slow, Quick, Quick

MAN'S PART: Forward

1. Left foot forward, Slow
2. Right foot forward, Slow (use straight follow-through)
3. Left foot forward and to side, Quick (use straight follow-through)
4. Close with right foot, Quick

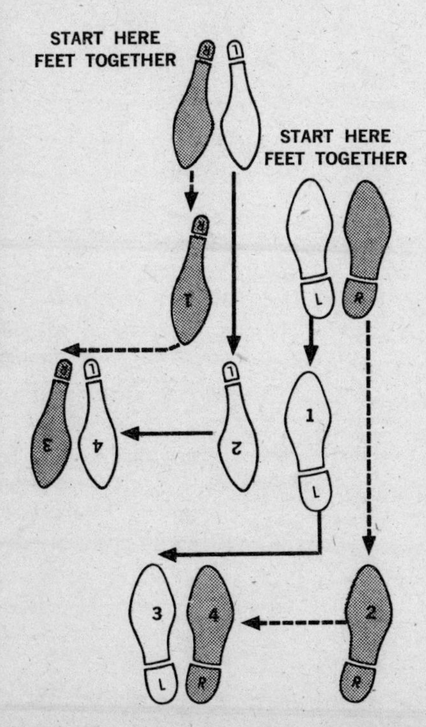

MAN'S PART: Backward

1. Left foot backward, Slow
2. Right foot backward, Slow (use straight follow-through)
3. Left foot backward and to side, Quick (use straight follow-through)
4. Close with right foot, Quick

NOTE: This step is danced in the closed position.

GIRL'S PART: Forward

1. Right foot forward, Slow
2. Left foot forward, Slow (use straight follow-through)
3. Right foot forward and to side, Quick (use straight follow-through)
4. Close with left foot, Quick

NOTE: See note under man's part.

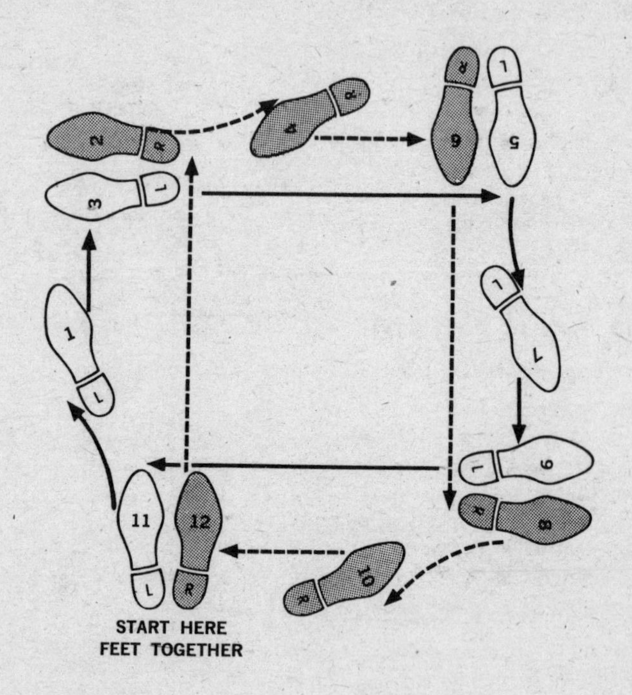

LEFT TURN

Rhythm: Slow, Quick, Quick
Slow, Quick, Quick

MAN'S PART:

1. Left foot forward, Slow (turn toe slightly outward)
2. Right foot forward and to side, Quick
3. Close with left foot, Quick (feet are parallel)
4. Right foot backward, Slow (turn toe slightly inward)
5. Left foot backward and to side, Quick
6. Close with right foot, Quick (feet are parallel)
7. Left foot forward, Slow (turn toe slightly outward)
8. Right foot forward and to side, Quick
9. Close with left foot, Quick (feet are parallel)
10. Right foot backward, Slow (turn toe slightly inward)
11. Left foot backward and to side Quick
12. Close with right foot, Quick (feet are parallel)

NOTE: Turn gradually to the left, making a quarter turn between steps 1 and 3 and a quarter turn between steps 4 and 6. Steps 7 through 12 are a repeat of steps 1 through 6.

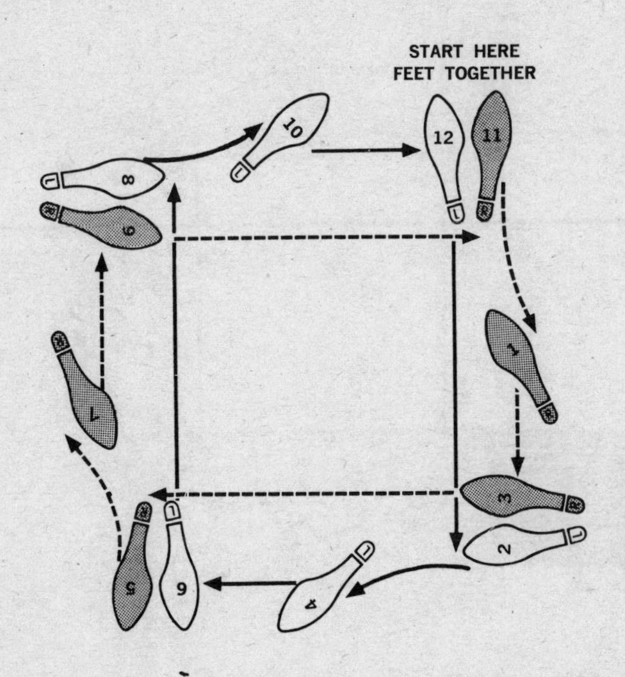

LEFT TURN

Rhythm: Slow, Quick, Quick
Slow, Quick, Quick

GIRL'S PART:

1. Right foot backward, Slow (turn toe slightly inward)
2. Left foot backward and to side, Quick
3. Close with right foot, Quick (feet are parallel)
4. Left foot forward, Slow (turn toe slightly outward)
5. Right foot forward and to side, Quick
6. Close with left foot, Quick (feet are parallel)
7. Right foot backward, Slow (turn toe slightly inward)
8. Left foot backward and to side, Quick
9. Close with right foot, Quick (feet are parallel)
10. Left foot forward, Slow (turn toe slightly outward)
11. Right foot forward and to side, Quick
12. Close with left foot, Quick (feet are parallel)

NOTE: See note under man's part.

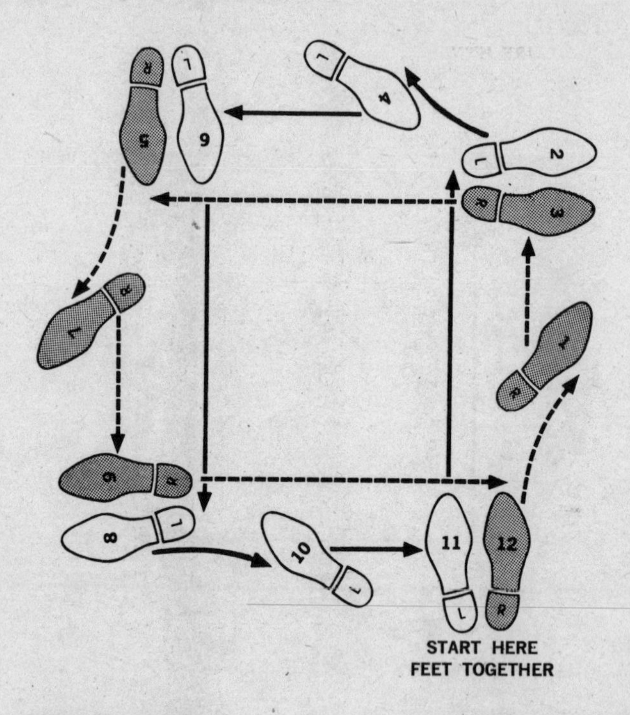

RIGHT TURN

Rhythm: Slow, Quick, Quick
Slow, Quick, Quick

MAN'S PART:

1. Right foot forward, Slow (turn toe slightly outward)
2. Left foot forward and to side, Quick
3. Close with right foot, Quick (feet are parallel)
4. Left foot backward, Slow (turn toe slightly inward)
5. Right foot backward and to side, Quick
6. Close with left foot, Quick (feet are parallel)
7. Right foot forward, Slow (turn toe slightly outward)
8. Left foot forward and to side, Quick
9. Close with right foot, Quick (feet are parallel)
10. Left foot backward, Slow (turn toe slightly inward)
11. Right foot backward and to side, Quick
12. Close with left foot, Quick (feet are parallel)

NOTE: When actually dancing with a partner, first take one forward or backward step with your left foot, then start the right-turn pattern on your right foot; or you may dance steps 1, 2 and 3 of the One-Step, and then begin. Apply the same principles of turning as outlined for the Left Turn.

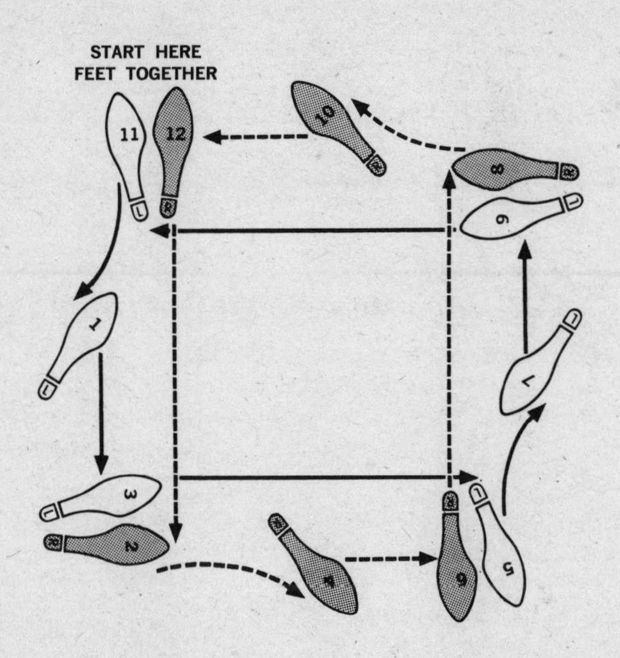

RIGHT TURN

Rhythm: Slow, Quick, Quick
Slow, Quick, Quick

GIRL'S PART:

1. Left foot backward, Slow (turn toe slightly inward)
2. Right foot backward and to side, Quick
3. Close with left foot, Quick (feet are parallel)
4. Right foot forward, Slow (turn toe slightly outward)
5. Left foot forward and to side, Quick
6. Close with right foot, Quick (feet are parallel)
7. Left foot backward, Slow (turn toe slightly inward)
8. Right foot backward and to side,
9. Close with left foot, Quick (feet are parallel)
10. Right foot forward, Slow (turn toe slightly outward)
11. Left foot forward and to side, Quick
12. Close with right foot, Quick (feet are parallel)

NOTE: When actually dancing with a partner, first take one backward or forward step with your right foot, then start the right-turn pattern on your left foot; or you may dance steps 1, 2, and 3 of the One-Step, then begin. Apply the same principles of turning as outlined for the Left Turn.

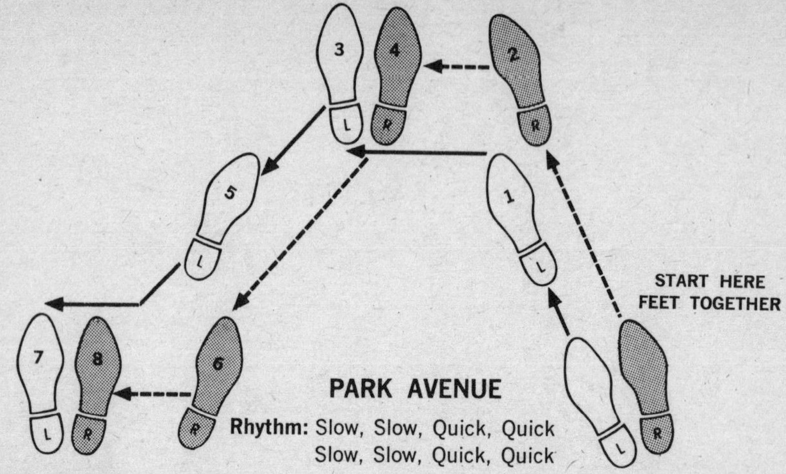

PARK AVENUE

Rhythm: Slow, Slow, Quick, Quick
Slow, Slow, Quick, Quick

MAN'S PART

1. Left foot forward, Slow
2. Right foot forward, Slow
3. Left foot forward and to side, Quick
4. Close with right foot, Quick
5. Left foot backward diagonal, Slow
6. Right foot backward, Slow
7. Left foot backward and to side, Quick
8. Close with right foot, Quick

NOTE: When dancing with a partner, the entire pattern can be danced in the closed position; or steps 1 and 2 may be danced in the right side position, steps 3 and 4 in the closed position, steps 5 and 6 in the left side position, and steps 7 and 8 in the closed position. Review Chapter 10, "The Dance Positions."

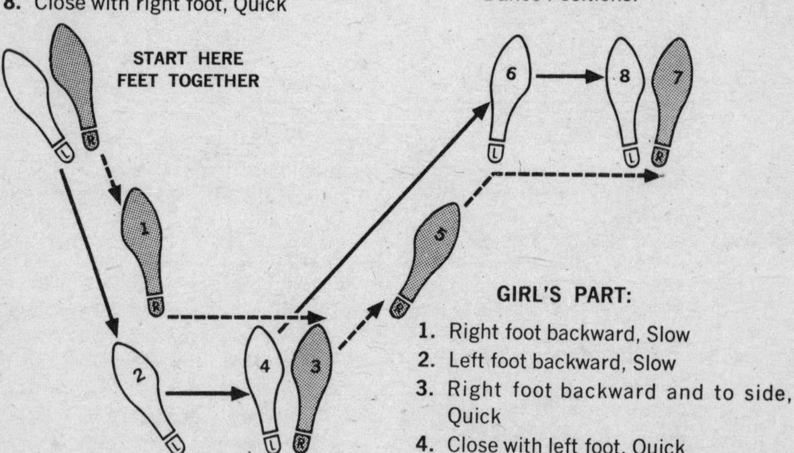

PARK AVENUE

Rhythm: Slow, Slow, Quick, Quick
Slow, Slow, Quick, Quick

GIRL'S PART:

1. Right foot backward, Slow
2. Left foot backward, Slow
3. Right foot backward and to side, Quick
4. Close with left foot, Quick
5. Right foot forward diagonal, Slow
6. Left foot forward, Slow
7. Right foot forward and to side, Quick
8. Close with left foot, Quick

NOTE: See note under man's part.

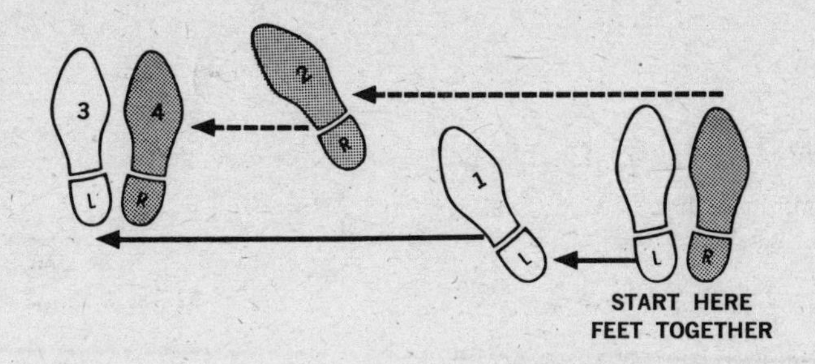

THREE LITTLE WORDS

Rhythm: Slow, Slow, Quick, Quick

MAN'S PART:

1. Left foot to side with toe out, Slow
2. Right foot in front of left foot, Slow
3. Left foot to side, Quick
4. Close with right foot, Quick

NOTE: Steps 1 and 2 are danced in the left open position, steps 3 and 4 in the closed position. Review Chapter 10, entitled "The Dance Positions."

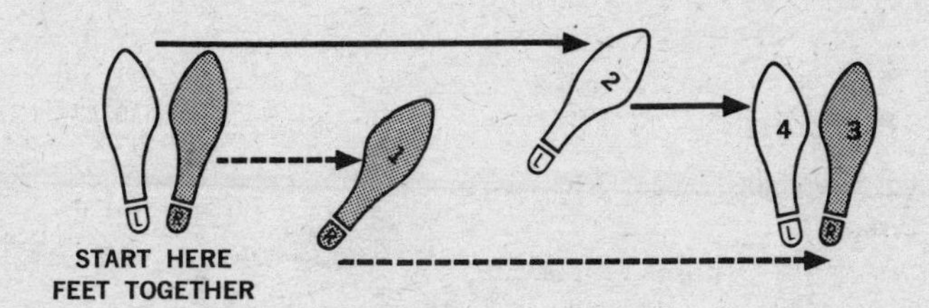

THREE LITTLE WORDS

Rhythm: Slow, Slow, Quick, Quick

GIRL'S PART:

1. Right foot to side with toe out, Slow
2. Left foot in front of right foot, Slow
3. Right foot to side, Quick
4. Close with left foot, Quick

NOTE: See note under man's part.

AD-LIB TURN TO LEFT

Rhythm: Slow, Slow, Quick, Quick

MAN'S PART:

1. Left foot forward, Slow (point toe slightly to left)
2. Right foot backward and slightly to side, Slow
3. Left foot to side, Quick (point toe so both feet are parallel)
4. Close with right foot, Quick

NOTE: Turn gradually to the left, making a quarter turn between steps 1 and 2. This step may be repeated as many times as desired. The Ad-Lib is extremely useful when another couple blocks your line of progression.

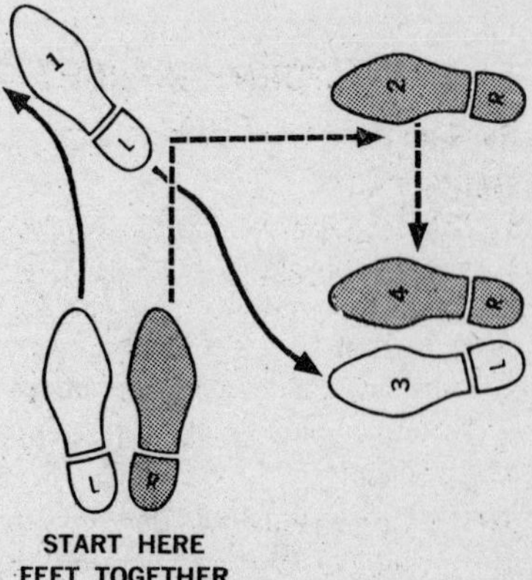

AD-LIB TURN TO LEFT

Rhythm: Slow, Slow, Quick, Quick

GIRL'S PART:

1. Right foot backward, Slow (point toe slightly to left)
2. Left foot forward and slightly to side, Slow
3. Right foot to side, Quick (point toe so both feet are parallel)
4. Close with left foot, Quick

NOTE: See note under man's part.

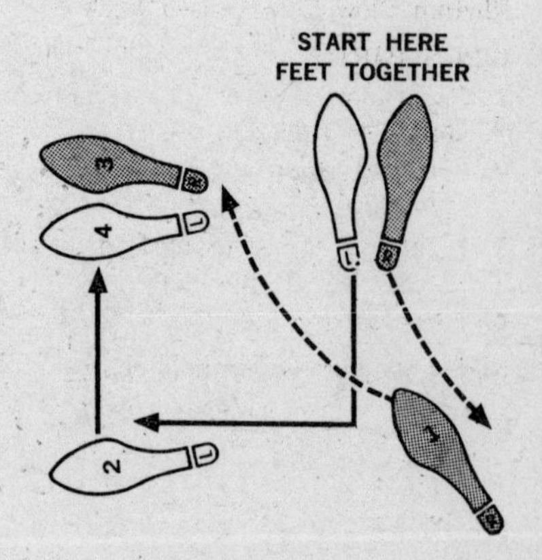

AD-LIB TURN TO RIGHT

Rhythm: Slow, Slow, Quick, Quick

MAN'S PART:

1. Left foot backward, Slow (point toe slightly to right)
2. Right foot forward and slightly to side, Slow
3. Left foot to side, Quick (point toe so both feet are parallel)
4. Close with right foot, Quick

NOTE: Turn gradually to the right, making a quarter turn between steps 1 and 2.

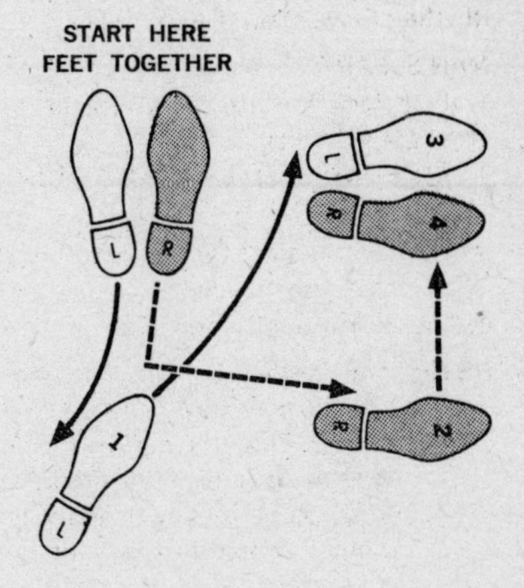

AD-LIB TURN TO RIGHT

Rhythm: Slow, Slow, Quick, Quick

GIRL'S PART:

1. Right foot forward, Slow (point toe slightly to right)
2. Left foot backward and slightly to side, Slow
3. Right foot to side, Quick (point toe so both feet are parallel)
4. Close with left foot, Quick

NOTE: See note under man's part.

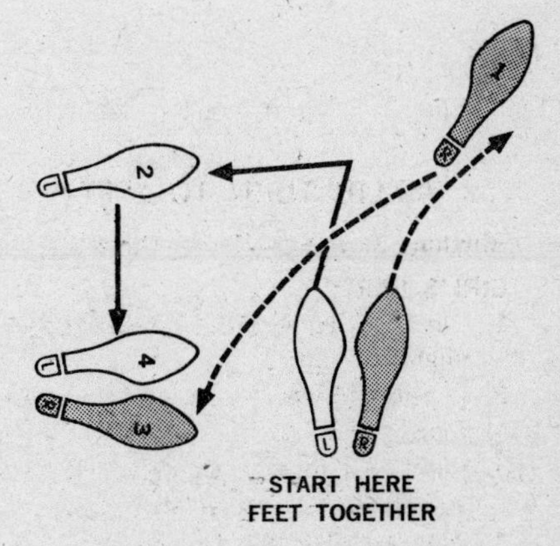

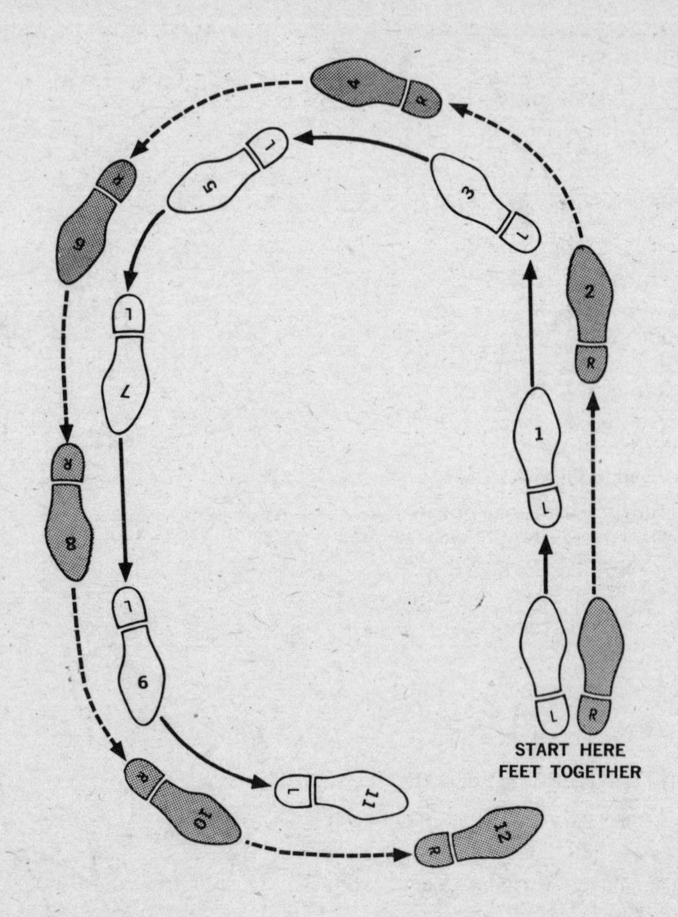

RUNNING STEPS

Rhythm: Slow, Quick, Quick
Slow, Quick, Quick

MAN'S PART:

1. Left foot forward, Slow
2. Right foot forward, Quick
3. Left foot forward, Quick (start turn to left)
4. Right foot forward, Slow
5. Left foot forward, Quick
6. Right foot forward, Quick
7. Left foot forward, Slow
8. Right foot forward, Quick
9. Left foot forward, Quick
10. Right foot forward, Slow
11. Left foot forward, Quick
12. Right foot forward, Quick (complete turn to left)

NOTE: The Running Steps can be turned gradually or sharply according to the size and shape of your room. You can also do the Running Steps in a straight line, with no turn.

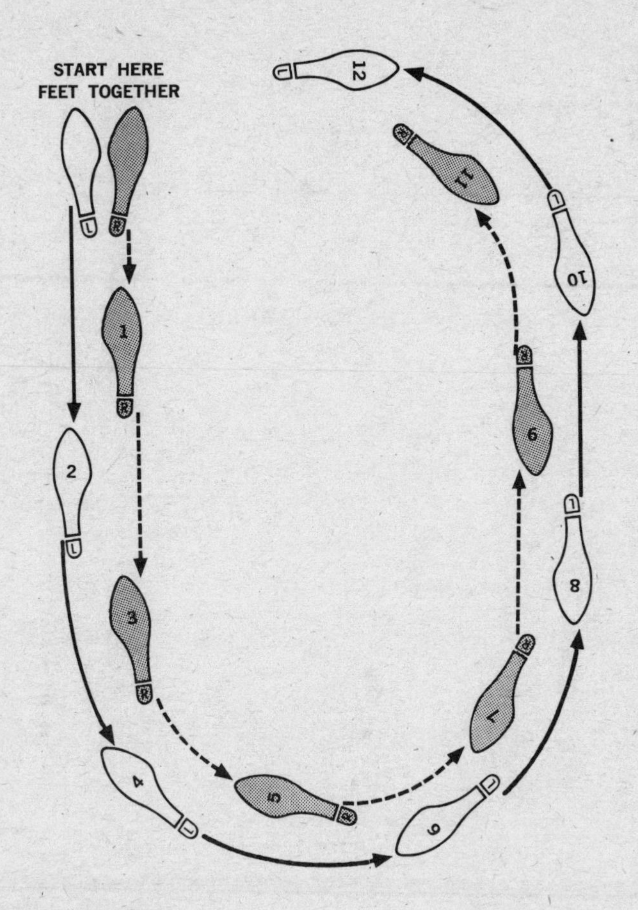

RUNNING STEPS

Rhythm: Slow, Quick, Quick
Slow, Quick, Quick

GIRL'S PART:

1. Right foot backward, Slow
2. Left foot backward, Quick
3. Right foot backward, Quick (start turn to left)
4. Left foot backward, Slow
5. Right foot backward, Quick
6. Left foot backward, Quick
7. Right foot backward, Slow
8. Left foot backward, Quick
9. Right foot backward, Quick
10. Left foot backward, Slow
11. Right foot backward, Quick
12. Left foot backward, Quick (complete turn to left)

NOTE: See note under man's part.

OPEN TWINKLE

Rhythm: Slow, Quick, Quick
Slow, Quick, Quick

MAN'S PART:

1. Left foot forward, Slow
2. Right foot forward and to side, Quick (point toe slightly to left)
3. Close with left foot, Quick
4. Right foot forward, Slow
5. Left foot forward and to side, Quick (point toe slightly to right)
6. Close with right foot, Quick

NOTE: The Open Twinkle is a slight variation of the basic One Step. As the left foot closes to the right foot (step 3), the man leads his partner to turn slightly, so that both partners are in the left open position. Steps 5 and 6 are danced in the closed position. (See drawings.)

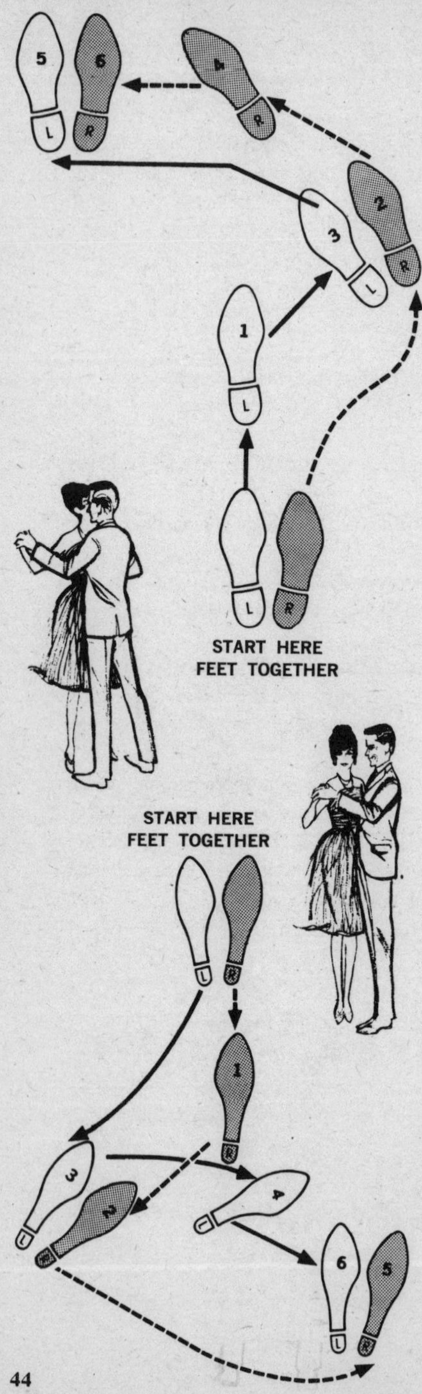

OPEN TWINKLE

Rhythm: Slow, Quick, Quick
Slow, Quick, Quick

GIRL'S PART:

1. Right foot backward, Slow
2. Left foot backward and to side, Quick (turn toe slightly to right)
3. Close with right foot, Quick
4. Left foot forward, across front of right foot, Slow
5. Right foot side, Quick (point toe slightly to left)
6. Close with left foot, Quick

NOTE: See note under man's part.

Astaire Styling: The Side Rock

Now that you have studied the step patterns for the Fox Trot and can dance them rhythmically to music, you are ready to apply the finishing touch to your technique—the proper body motion. Styling is the most attractive and harmonious motion of the upper body in relation to the feet. This use of the entire body affords today's natural, relaxed look that is so characteristic of the technique taught at the Fred Astaire Dance Studios. In the Fox Trot, which more than any other dance typifies the Fred Astaire style of movement, this special body motion is called the "side rock" or "side sway."

As the name implies, the side rock is used whenever you take a step to the side. The side rock is a very definite styling point that you should at first execute consciously and purposefully:

1. Start with feet apart.

2. Shift the torso to the left side, at the same time letting your body weight rest entirely on the left foot.

3. Lower your left shoulder slightly, still keeping your weight on the left foot.

4. Return to starting position.

5. Shift the torso to the right side, placing your weight on the right foot.

6. Lower your right shoulder slightly, still supporting your weight on the right foot.

Now try dancing the side rock once more, first to the left, then to the right. Keep both feet flat on the floor in the beginning, until you can execute the motion gracefully. Remember to move only the upper portion of your body. Relax your knees so that they are slightly flexed.

At first, you will probably find it necessary to exaggerate the shifting of your torso, but with more practice you will be able to subdue the motion until only a pleasing sway is evident. When you are confident that you can do the side rock garcefully in place, try it while dancing the One Step and eventually other patterns in the Fox Trot. Blend the body motion with your side steps. When you can do this, the Fox Trot will appear to be a relaxed and effortless dance.

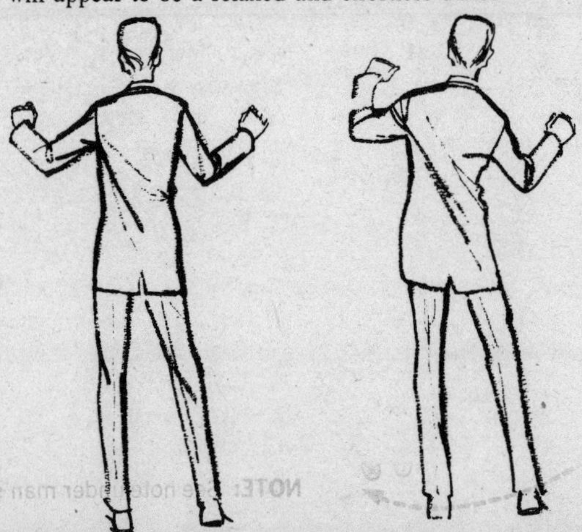

FOX TROT COMBINATIONS

Pattern	Number of Steps	Rhythm
(A)		
Basic Astaire Two Step	8	Slow, Slow, Quick, Quick
Open Twinkle	6	Slow, Quick, Quick
Running Steps	12	Slow, Quick, Quick
(B)		
Left Turn	12	All Steps: Slow, Quick, Quick
Basic Astaire One Step	3	
Right Turn	12	
Basic Astaire One Step	3	
(C)		
Basic Astaire Two Step	4	Slow, Slow, Quick, Quick
Park Avenue	8	Slow, Slow, Quick, Quick
Three Little Words	4	Slow, Slow, Quick, Quick
Open Twinkle	6	Slow, Quick, Quick

CHAPTER FIFTEEN

The American Waltz

INTRODUCTION

WHEN the Waltz was first introduced in the early nineteenth century, people were shocked. A man dancing with his hand upon a lady's waist? No proper young maiden would compromise herself so. The Waltz was thought to be a wicked, wicked thing.

Originating in the country folk dances of Bavaria, the Waltz did not become popular among the European middle class until the first decade of the twentieth century. Until then, it was the cherished property of the aristocracy. Yet in the United States, where there was no blue-blood caste, it was being danced by the citizenry as early as 1840. Immediately upon its introduction in this country, the Waltz became one of the most popular of all American dances; it later proved its mettle by being the only dance to survive the "ragtime revolution."

With the beginning of ragtime in 1910, the Waltz slipped into second place in the public's fancy, being supplanted by the many walking, strutting dances of that era. People who had not mastered the techniques and whirling patterns of the Waltz quickly learned the simple walking patterns, and so came the great ragtime rage and the birth of the Fox Trot.

In the latter part of the nineteenth century, composers were writing Waltzes to a slower tempo than that of the original Viennese style. "After the Ball" and "The Band Played On" are two Waltzes characteristic of this era. The box step, typical of the American Waltz, was being taught in the 1880s, and an even slower Waltz came into prominence in the early 1920s. The result is that we have three distinct tempos: (1) the fast or Viennese Waltz, (2) the medium Waltz, and (3) the slow Waltz—the last two being of American invention. Lately, there has been a revival of interest in the Waltz, and many people are discovering the joy of dancing to the invigorating music of Lehar, Strauss, and Chopin.

The Waltz is easy and flowing. Though it has been likened to the Fox Trot, it sustains a more delicate sweeping and gliding movement. If you wish, you can easily adapt some of the steps you learned in the Fox Trot to Waltz rhythm. When you have mastered all the Waltz patterns given here, go back to the Fox Trot and apply Waltz rhythm to the Left Turn, Right Turn, and Open Twinkle. There is no explanation of rhythm in any of the Waltz diagrams because every step is taken to one beat of music—Quick, Quick, Quick.

Remember to dance with your entire body. All side steps in the Waltz should be long and wide in order to obtain control and fluidity of movement. Keep your knees flexed; never let them lock so your leg moves stiffly. However, when the step patterns indicate that you bring your feet together or cross them, your knees will not be as flexed as otherwise.

Use straight follow-through when progressing forward or backward and curved follow-through before stepping to the side. Reread Chapter 11, Section II, entitled "Follow-Through," if you are not sure of the meaning of these terms.

Many people make the mistake of dancing on their toes throughout the Waltz. This is both tiring and incorrect. The first step in any pattern should be taken on the flat of the foot. The remaining two steps will take care of themselves.

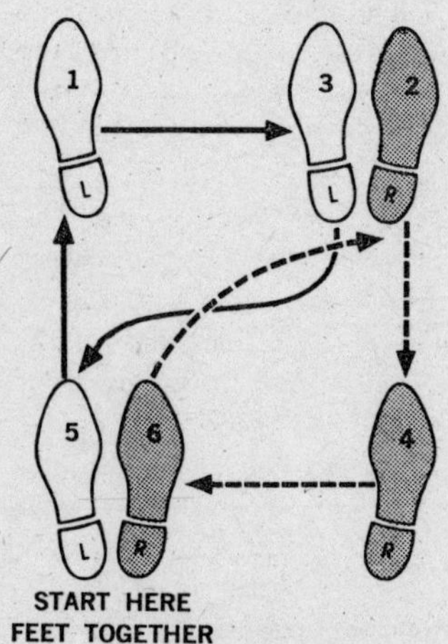

BASIC BOX STEP

Rhythm Count: ONE, Two, Three
ONE, Two, Three

MAN'S PART:

1. Left foot forward
2. Right foot forward and to side
3. Close with left foot
4. Right foot backward
5. Left foot backward and to side
6. Close with right foot

NOTE: Use the curved follow-through before moving to the side. Review Chapter 11, "Follow-Through."

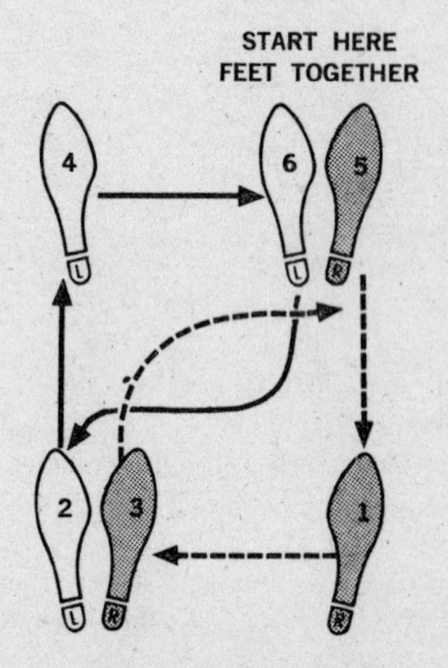

BASIC BOX STEP

Rhythm Count: ONE, Two, Three
ONE, Two, Three

GIRL'S PART:

1. Right foot backward
2. Left foot backward and to side
3. Close with right foot
4. Left foot forward
5. Right foot forward and to side
6. Close with left foot

NOTE: See note under man's part.

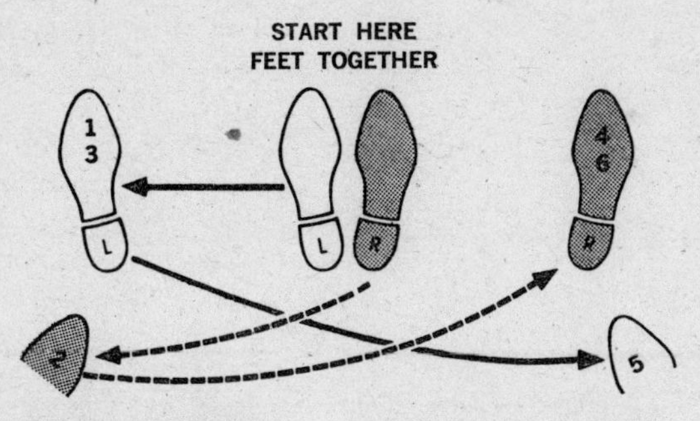

CROSS BALANCE STEPS

Rhythm Count: ONE, Two, Three
ONE, Two, Three

MAN'S PART:

1. Left foot to side
2. Right foot behind left foot (put weight on ball of foot)
3. Left foot in place
4. Right foot forward and to side
5. Left foot behind right foot (put weight on ball of foot)
6. Right foot in place

NOTE: The Cross Balance Step is a slight variation of the Balance Step Side to Side. Instead of closing the foot on the 2nd and 5th steps, cross it slightly behind the supporting leg and place weight on it. Maintain the closed position throughout.

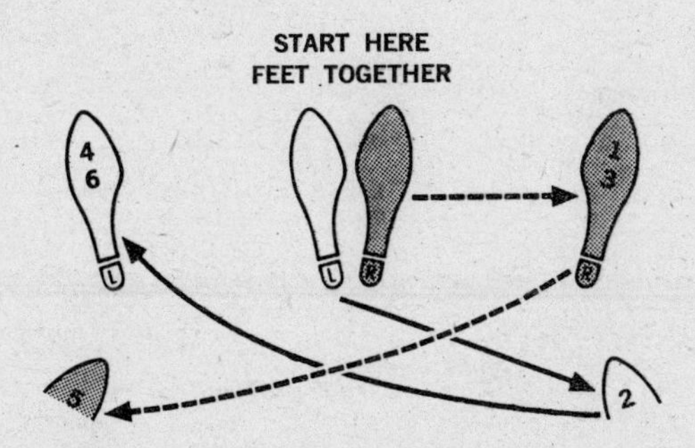

CROSS BALANCE STEPS

Rhythm Count: ONE, Two, Three
ONE, Two, Three

GIRL'S PART:

1. Right foot to side
2. Left foot behind right foot (put weight on ball of foot)
3. Right foot in place
4. Left foot forward and to side
5. Right foot behind left foot (put weight on ball of foot)
6. Left foot in place

NOTE: See note under man's part.

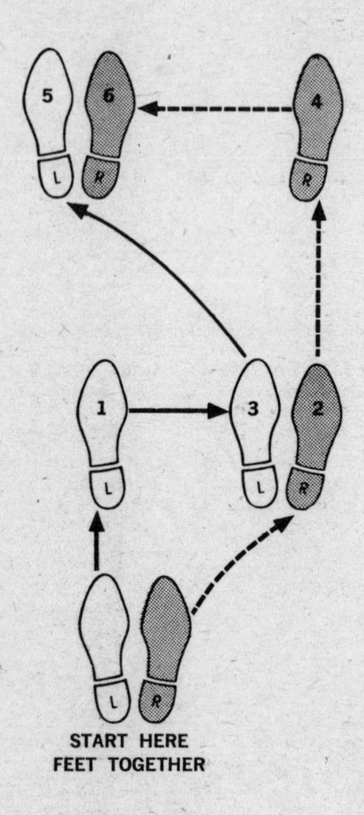

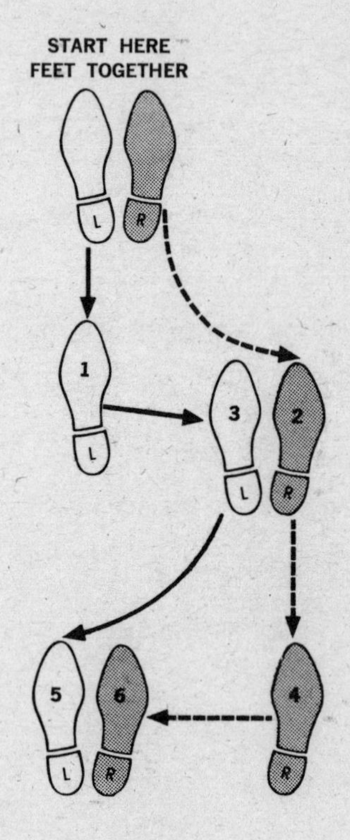

PROGRESSIVE BASIC

Rhythm Count: ONE, Two, Three
ONE, Two, Three

MAN'S PART: Forward

1. Left foot forward
2. Right foot forward and to side
3. Close with left foot
4. Right foot forward
5. Left foot forward and to side
6. Close with right foot

MAN'S PART: Backward

1. Left foot backward
2. Right foot backward and to side
3. Close with left foot
4. Right foot backward
5. Left foot backward and to side
6. Close with right foot.

NOTE: Use the curved follow-through before moving to the side. The Progressive Basic may be danced as many times as desired.

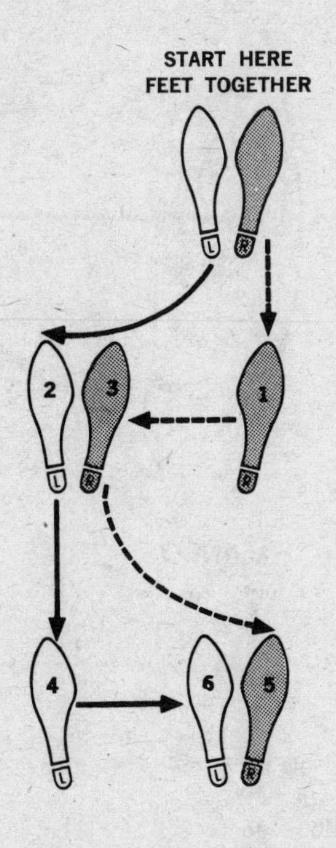

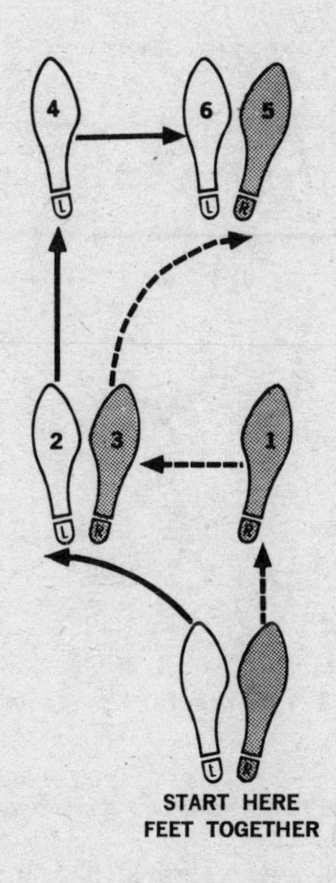

PROGRESSIVE BASIC

Rhythm Count: ONE, Two, Three
ONE, Two, Three

GIRL'S PART: Backward

1. Right foot backward
2. Left foot backward and to side
3. Close with right foot
4. Left foot backward
5. Right foot backward and to side
6. Close with left foot

GIRL'S PART: Forward

1. Right foot forward
2. Left foot forward and to side
3. Close with right foot
4. Left foot forward
5. Right foot forward and to side
6. Close with left foot

NOTE: See note under man's part.

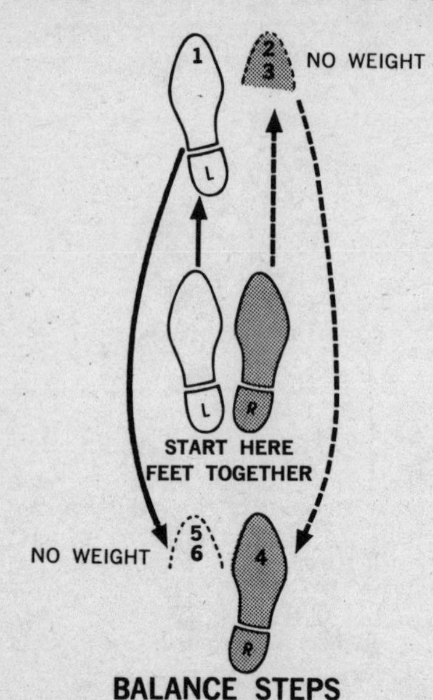

BALANCE STEPS

Rhythm Count: ONE, Two, Three
ONE, Two, Three

MAN'S PART: Forward and Backward

1. Left foot forward
2. Right foot forward, closing to left (simply touch toe, putting no weight on right foot)
3. Hold right foot in place (still putting no weight on right foot)
4. Right foot backward
5. Left foot backward, closing to right (simply touch toe, putting no weight on left foot)
6. Hold left foot in place (still putting no weight on left foot)

NOTE: Balance Steps are danced in place when you do not wish to progress around the dance floor, or when another couple is in your path, or at the beginning of a dance to pick up the proper tempo. You may repeat the step or, starting on your left foot, begin any other Waltz pattern. Balance Steps are danced in closed position.

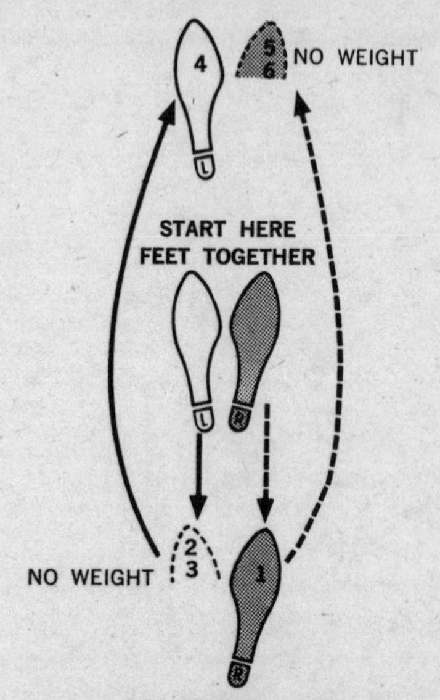

BALANCE STEPS

Rhythm Count: ONE, Two, Three
ONE, Two, Three

GIRL'S PART: Backward and Forward

1. Right foot backward
2. Left foot backward, closing to right (simply touch toe, putting no weight on left foot)
3. Hold left foot in place (still putting no weight on left foot)
4. Left foot forward
5. Right foot forward, closing to left (simply touch toe, putting no weight on right foot)
6. Hold right foot in place (still putting no weight on right foot)

NOTE: The man uses Balance Steps when he wishes to dance in place and not progress around the dance floor. He may repeat it any number of times or lead you into a new pattern, which you will begin on your right foot.

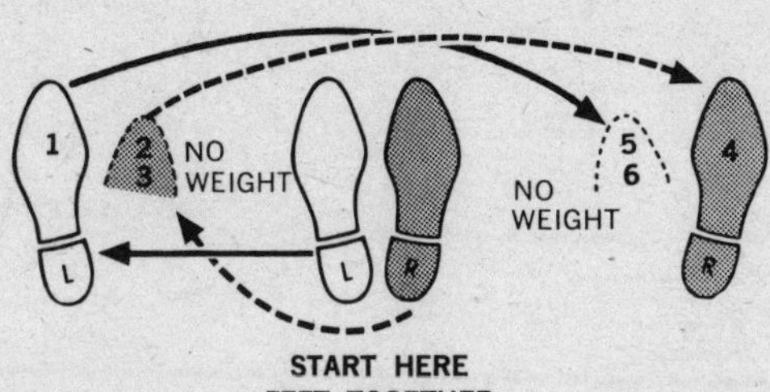

BALANCE STEPS

Rhythm Count: ONE, Two, Three
ONE, Two, Three

MAN'S PART: Side to Side

1. Left foot to side
2. Close with right foot (simply touch toe to floor, putting no weight on right foot)
3. Hold in place
4. Right foot to side
5. Close with left foot (simply touch toe to floor, putting no weight on left foot)
6. Hold in place

NOTE: See note for Balance Steps, Forward and Backward.

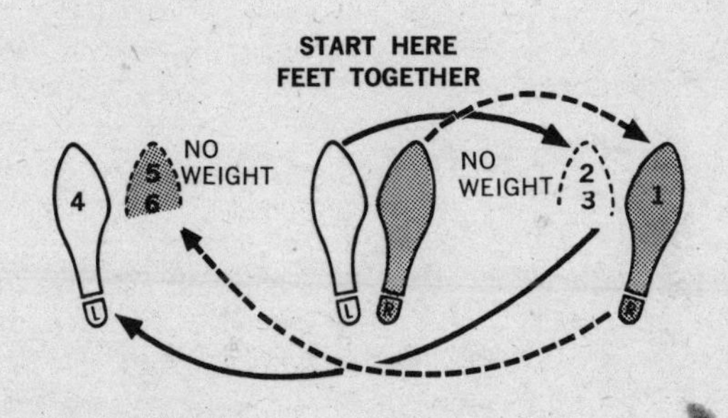

BALANCE STEPS

Rhythm Count: ONE, Two, Three
ONE, Two, Three

GIRL'S PART: Side to Side

1. Right foot to side
2. Close with left foot (simply touch toe to floor, putting no weight on left foot)
3. Hold in place
4. Left foot to side
5. Close with right foot (simply touch toe to floor, putting no weight on right foot)
6. Hold in place

NOTE: See note for Balance Steps, Backward and Forward.

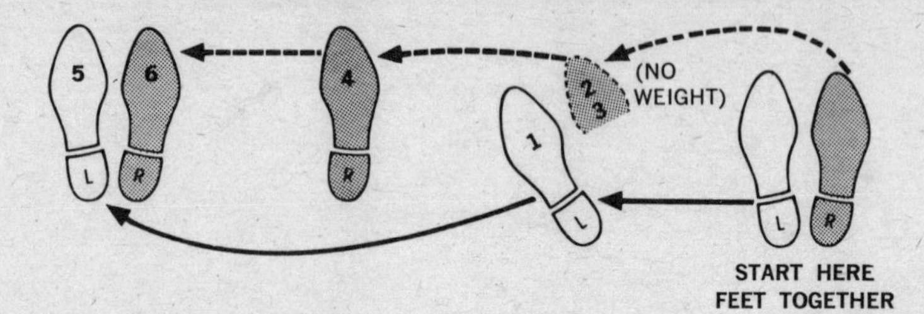

THREE LITTLE WORDS

Rhythm Count: ONE, Two, Three
ONE, Two, Three

MAN'S PART:

1. Left foot to side (point toe slightly outward)
2. Close with right foot (simply touch toe to floor, putting no weight on right foot)
3. Hold right foot in place (still putting no weight on right foot)
4. Right foot forward (cross in front of left foot)
5. Left foot to side
6. Close with right foot

NOTE: Three Little Words combines a Forward Balance Step and a Forward Waltz Step; however, the pattern is danced starting in the left open dance position. Only steps 5 and 6 are in closed position. Refer to Chapter 10, "The Dance Positions."

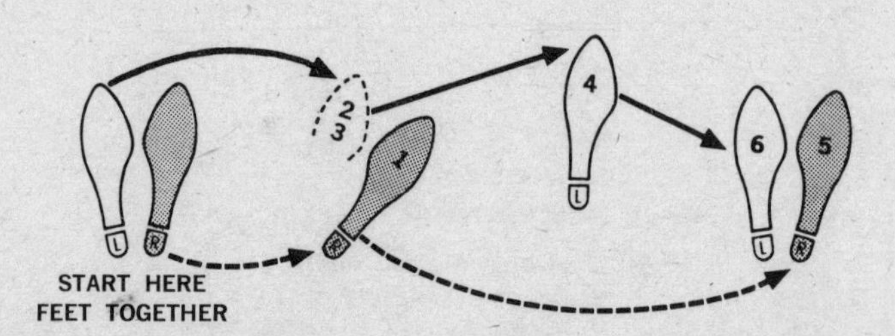

THREE LITTLE WORDS

Rhythm Count: ONE, Two, Three
ONE, Two, Three

GIRL'S PART:

1. Right foot to side (point toe slightly outward)
2. Close with left foot (simply touch toe to floor, putting no weight on left foot)
3. Hold left foot in place (still putting no weight on left foot)
4. Left foot forward (cross in front of right foot)
5. Right foot to side
6. Close with left foot

NOTE: See note under man's part.

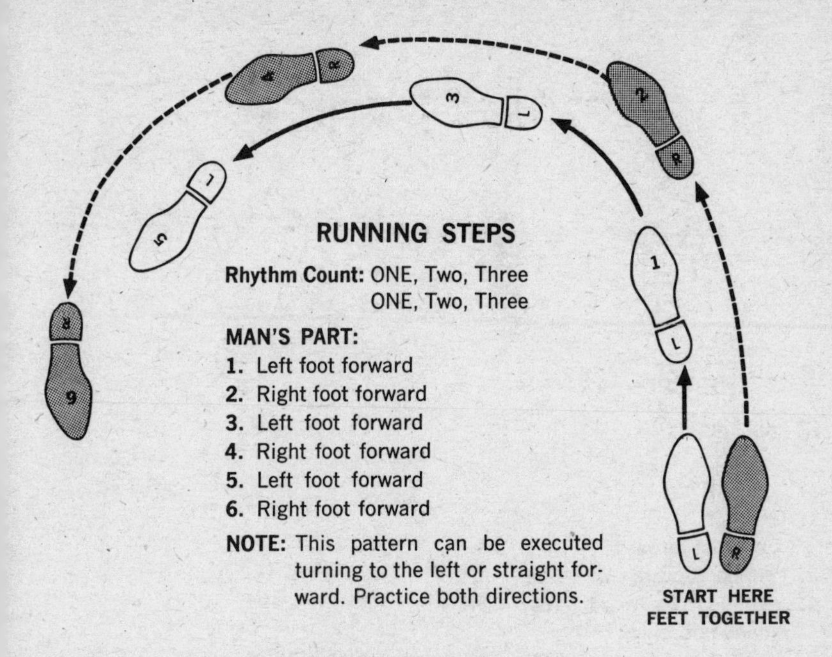

RUNNING STEPS

Rhythm Count: ONE, Two, Three
ONE, Two, Three

MAN'S PART:

1. Left foot forward
2. Right foot forward
3. Left foot forward
4. Right foot forward
5. Left foot forward
6. Right foot forward

NOTE: This pattern can be executed turning to the left or straight forward. Practice both directions.

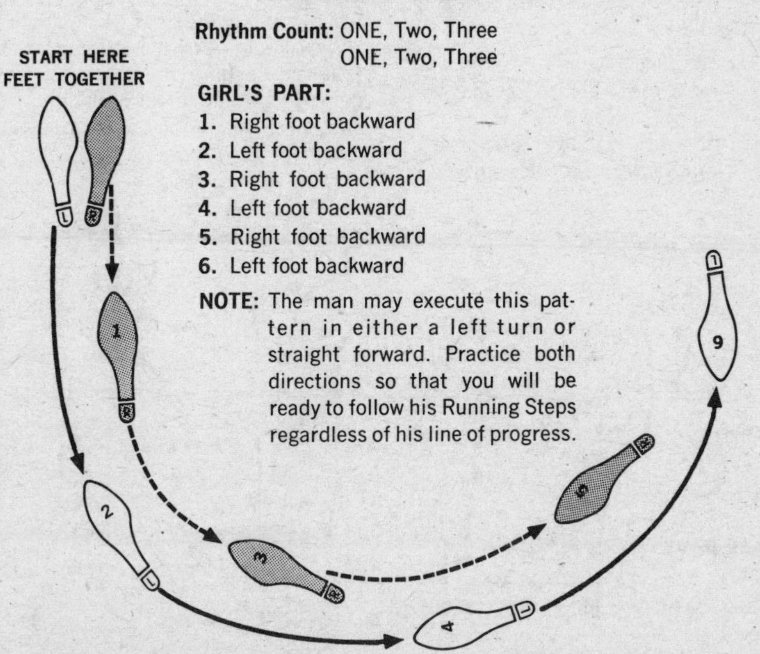

RUNNING STEPS

Rhythm Count: ONE, Two, Three
ONE, Two, Three

GIRL'S PART:

1. Right foot backward
2. Left foot backward
3. Right foot backward
4. Left foot backward
5. Right foot backward
6. Left foot backward

NOTE: The man may execute this pattern in either a left turn or straight forward. Practice both directions so that you will be ready to follow his Running Steps regardless of his line of progress.

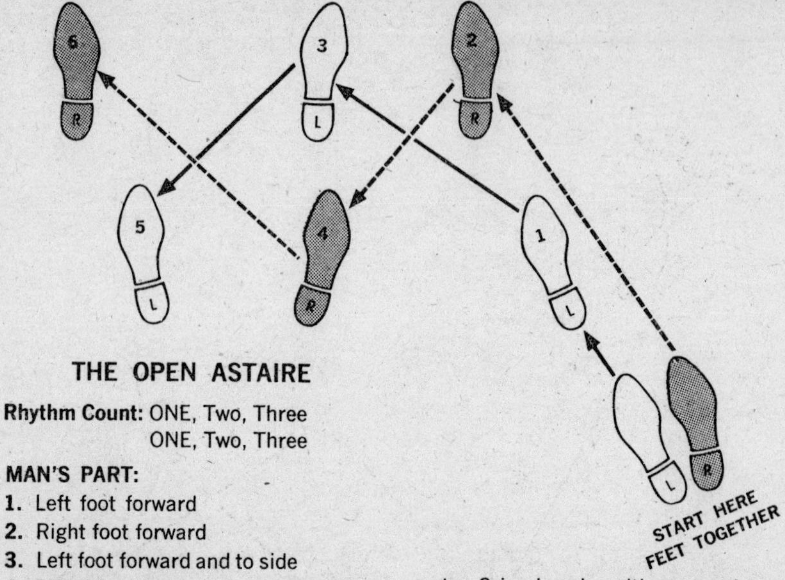

THE OPEN ASTAIRE

Rhythm Count: ONE, Two, Three
ONE, Two, Three

MAN'S PART:

1. Left foot forward
2. Right foot forward
3. Left foot forward and to side
4. Right foot backward (cross slightly behind left foot)
5. Left foot backward and to side
6. Right foot forward diagonal (crossing slightly in front of left foot)

NOTE: The Open Astaire is a popular variation which also may be danced in the Fox Trot. With a partner, steps 1 and 2 are danced in right side position, step 3 in closed position, step 4 in left side position, step 5 in closed position, and step 6 in right side position. The effect is that of weaving the steps forward and backward. After the 6th step is taken, continue forward with the left foot into closed position and dance one of the basic patterns. The girl will continue backward. (See drawings.)

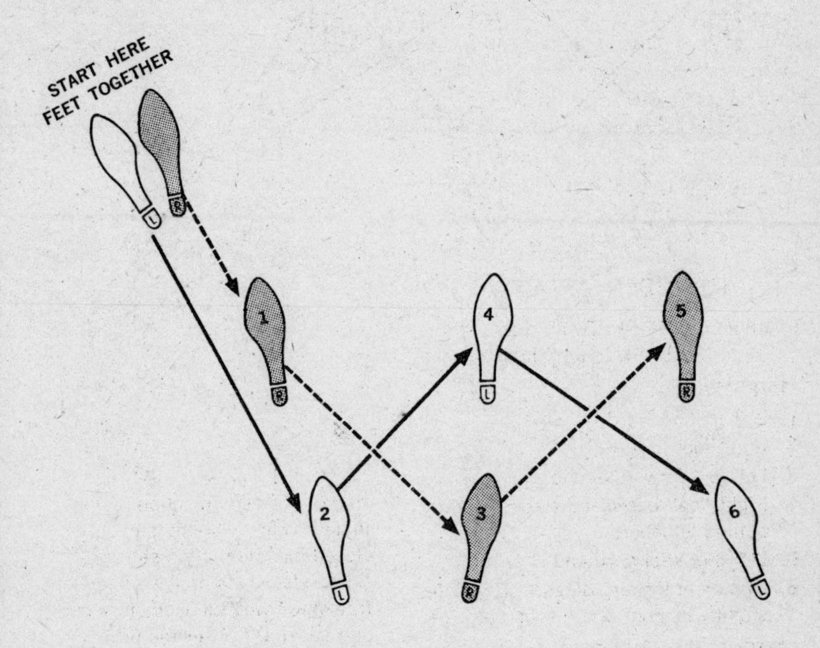

THE OPEN ASTAIRE

Rhythm Count: ONE, Two, Three
ONE, Two, Three

GIRL'S PART:

1. Right foot backward
2. Left foot backward
3. Right foot backward and to side
4. Left foot forward (cross slightly in front of right foot)
5. Right foot forward and to side
6. Left foot backward diagonal (crossing slightly behind right foot)

NOTE: See note under man's part.

THE ASTAIRE TWINKLES

Rhythm Count: ONE, Two, Three
ONE, Two, Three

MAN'S PART:

1. Left foot forward
2. Right foot forward and to side (point toe slightly inward)
3. Close with left foot
4. Right foot forward (point toe slightly outward)
5. Left foot forward and to side (point toe inward)
6. Close with right foot

NOTE: The Astaire Twinkles are a slight variation of the Progressive Basic. As the left foot closes (step 3), the man turns his partner slightly, so that both partners are in right side position. Step 4 is danced in right side position. As the right foot closes (step 6), the man turns his partner slightly, so that both partners are in left side position. This step can be repeated as many times as desired. When repeated, the first step is danced in left side position, rather than in closed position. (See drawings.)

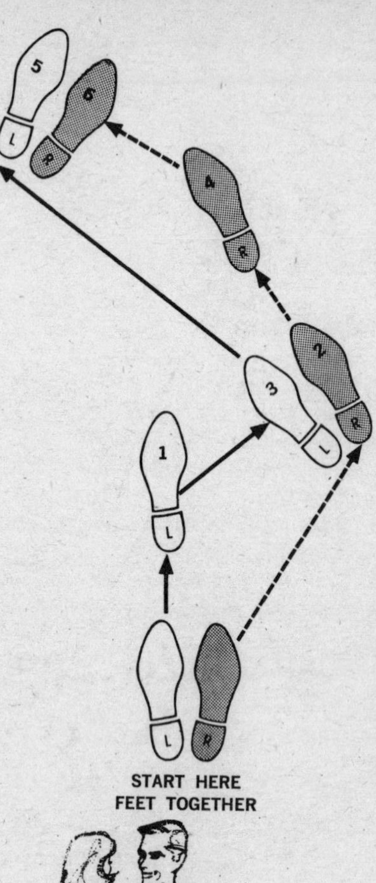

STEP 3

STEP 4

THE ASTAIRE TWINKLES

Rhythm Count: ONE, Two, Three
ONE, Two, Three

GIRL'S PART:

1. Right foot backward
2. Left foot backward and to side (point toe slightly outward)
3. Close with right foot
4. Left foot backward (point toe slightly inward)
5. Right foot backward and to side (point toe outward)
6. Close with left foot

NOTE: See note under man's part.

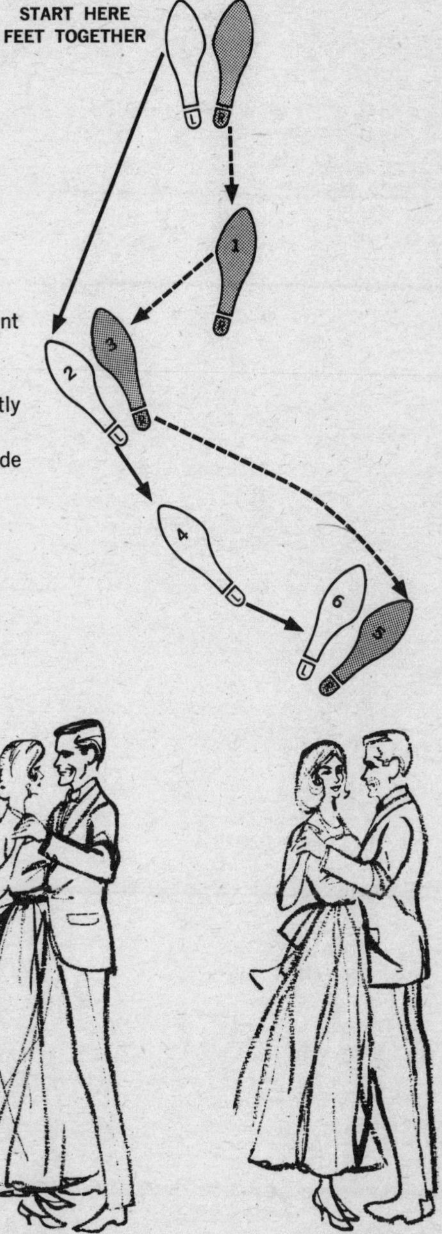

STEP 1

STEP 5

STEP 6

Astaire Styling: The Waltz Lilt

It is important to note that the strong ONE-Two-Three, ONE-Two-Three beat of the music contributes directly to the graceful body motion that should be utilized in dancing the waltz. Every movement of the torso, arms, and head should be inspired by this rhythm.

Because of the stress on the first beat, each should be taken with the knees slightly flexed and the foot flat on the floor. On the second and third beats, the knees gradually straighten, but are always kept as relaxed as possible. This knee action must be consistent, resulting in a fluid, lilting line. The knees act as shock absorbers and keep your body from bouncing up and down.

The rhythmic lilt of the Waltz should be executed with your upper body and not by changing the level of your feet. Stay light on your feet. Imagine, if you can, that you are dancing on a cloud and that a heavy step will cause you to fall through it. Remember to use the proper follow-through and to apply contrabody movement to all turning steps.

WALTZ COMBINATIONS

Pattern	Number of Steps	Rhythm and Count
(A)		
Progressive Basic	6	
Balance Steps—		All Quick Steps
Forward and Backward	4	Count: ONE, Two, Three
Balance Steps—		
Side to Side	4	
(B)		
The Astaire Twinkles	12	
Cross Balance Steps	6	All Quick Steps
Left Turn	12	Count, ONE, Two, Three
Running Steps	6	
(C)		
Progressive Basic	3	
Right Turn	3	All Quick Steps
Three Little Words	5	Count: ONE, Two, Three
The Astaire Twinkles	6	

CHAPTER SIXTEEN

The Cha Cha Cha

INTRODUCTION

THE name "Cha Cha Cha" comes from Cuba, where a few years ago the local musicians began chanting the syllable to compulsive triple rhythm. The Cha Cha Cha gathers its flavor, rhythm, and charm from three primary sources. It is a derivation of the Mambo, and therefore the Rumba, and it is also a stepchild of the Lindy, being danced to the same one-two-three triple step.

The Cha Cha Cha is a geographical half-breed, springing from Latin American roots and flowering under North American influence. While closely identified with the Mambo, the Cha Cha Cha has enough intrinsic individuality to be classified as a dance apart. The tempo is slow and staccato, much like a dramatic blues number. It is so much an on-the-beat dance that you can't help injecting your own personality into the patterns. This, perhaps more than anything else, makes the Cha Cha Cha a delight for inexperienced dancers. It is a real let-yourself-go kind of dance.

When learning the Cha Cha Cha, however, your footwork should be precise and sharp. Always be aware of your direction. This is not a smooth, flowing dance but rather a staccato, lively dance. Though the hip movements are similar to those of the Rumba, they are more syncopated and definite in style. Don't overexaggerate your hip movements so that you bounce up and down on the dance floor.

The Cha Cha Cha may be danced to either of two counts: One, Two, Cha-Cha-Cha (Quick, Quick, Quick And Quick) or One, Two, Three, Cha-Cha (Quick, Quick, Quick, Quick And). Both are described in the accompanying diagrams; however all breaks are written in the simpler One, Two, Cha-Cha-Cha count. When you get to the Advanced Basic Step, you can, if you wish, try all the previous patterns in this manner.

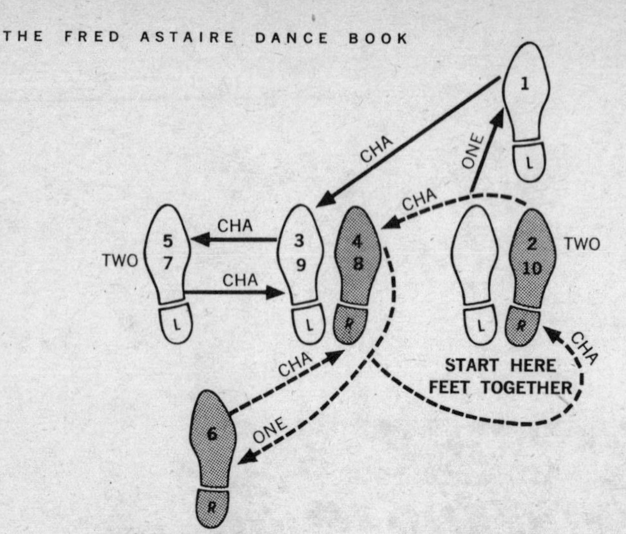

SIMPLE BASIC

Rhythm: One, Two, Cha-Cha-Cha
One, Two, Cha-Cha-Cha

MAN'S PART:

1. Left foot forward, Full Beat
2. Right foot in place, Full Beat
3. Left foot backward and to side, Half Beat
4. Close with right foot, Half Beat
5. Left foot to side, Full Beat
6. Right foot backward, Full Beat
7. Left foot in place, Full Beat
8. Right foot forward and to side, Half Beat
9. Close with left foot, Half Beat
10. Right foot to side, Full Beat

NOTE: This pattern is danced in closed position. Make footwork precise and take small steps.

SIMPLE BASIC

Rhythm: One, Two, Cha-Cha-Cha
One, Two, Cha-Cha-Cha

GIRL'S PART:

1. Right foot backward, Full Beat
2. Left foot in place, Full Beat
3. Right foot forward and to side, Half Beat
4. Close with left foot, Half Beat
5. Right foot to side, Full Beat
6. Left foot forward, Full Beat
7. Right foot in place, Full Beat
8. Left foot backward and to side, Half Beat
9. Close with left foot, Half Beat
10. Left foot to side, Full Beat

NOTE: See note under man's part.

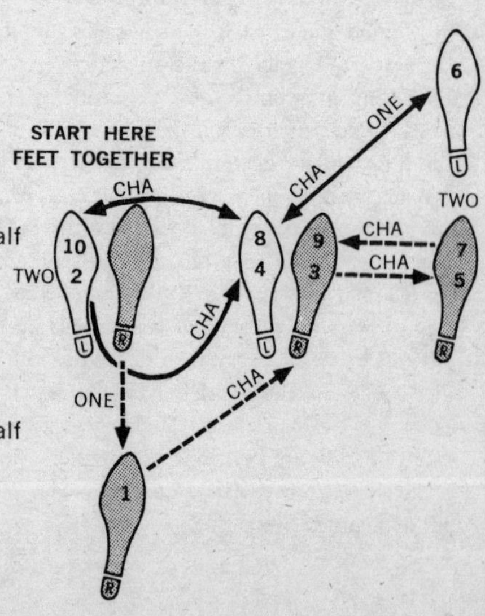

PROGRESSIVE BASIC

Rhythm: One, Two, Cha-Cha-Cha
One, Two, Cha-Cha-Cha

MAN'S PART:

1. Left foot forward, Full Beat
2. Right foot in place, Full Beat
3. Left foot backward, Half Beat
4. Right foot backward, Half Beat (small step)
5. Left foot backward, Full Beat
6. Right foot backward, Full Beat
7. Left foot in place, Full Beat
8. Right foot forward, Half Beat
9. Left foot forward, Half Beat (small step)
10. Right foot forward, Full Beat

NOTE: Take small steps on 3, 4, 5 and 8, 9, 10. The Progressive Basic is danced in the apart position.

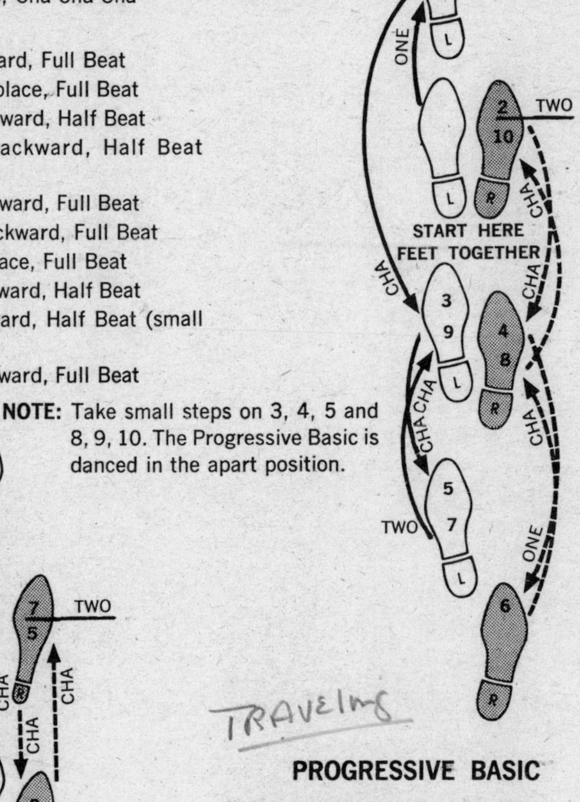

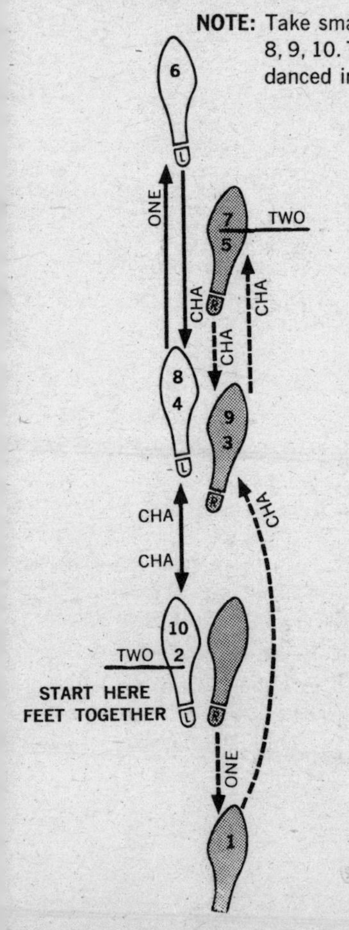

PROGRESSIVE BASIC

Rhythm: One, Two, Cha-Cha-Cha
One, Two, Cha-Cha-Cha

GIRL'S PART:

1. Right foot backward, Full Beat
2. Left foot in place, Full Beat
3. Right foot forward, Half Beat
4. Left foot forward, Half Beat (small step)
5. Right foot forward, Full Beat
6. Left foot forward, Full Beat
7. Right foot in place, Full Beat
8. Left foot backward, Half Beat
9. Right foot backward, Half Beat (small step)
10. Left foot backward, Full Beat

NOTE: See note under man's part.

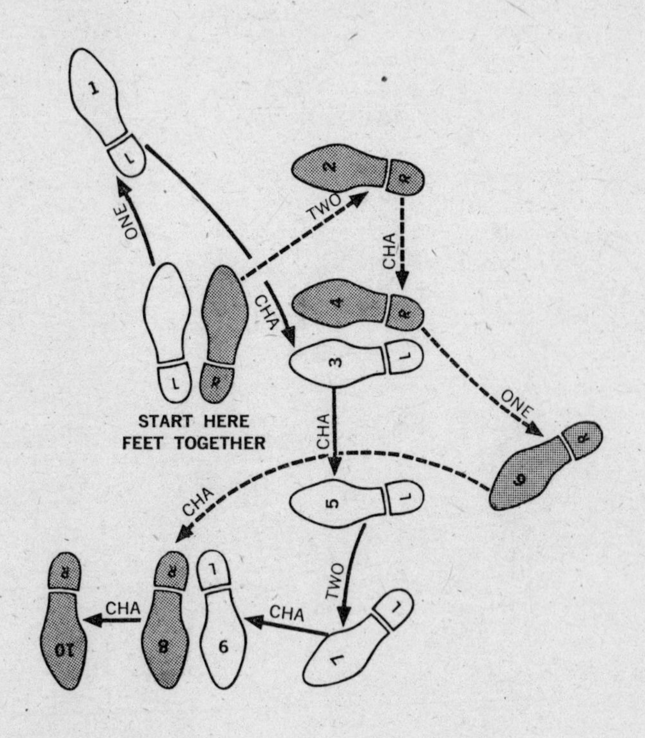

LEFT TURN

Rhythm: One, Two, Cha-Cha-Cha
One, Two, Cha-Cha-Cha

MAN'S PART:

1. Left foot forward, Full Beat
2. Right foot backward diagonal, Full Beat (point toe as shown in diagram)
3. Left foot backward and to side, Half Beat (point toe as shown, so feet are parallel)
4. Close with right foot, Half Beat
5. Left foot to side, Full Beat
6. Right foot backward, Full Beat (point toe as shown)
7. Left foot forward with toe out, Full Beat (point toe as shown)
8. Right foot forward and to side, Half Beat (point toe as shown)
9. Close with left foot, Half Beat
10. Right foot to side, Full Beat

NOTE: Turn gradually to the left, making a quarter turn between steps 1 and 2 and 6 and 7.

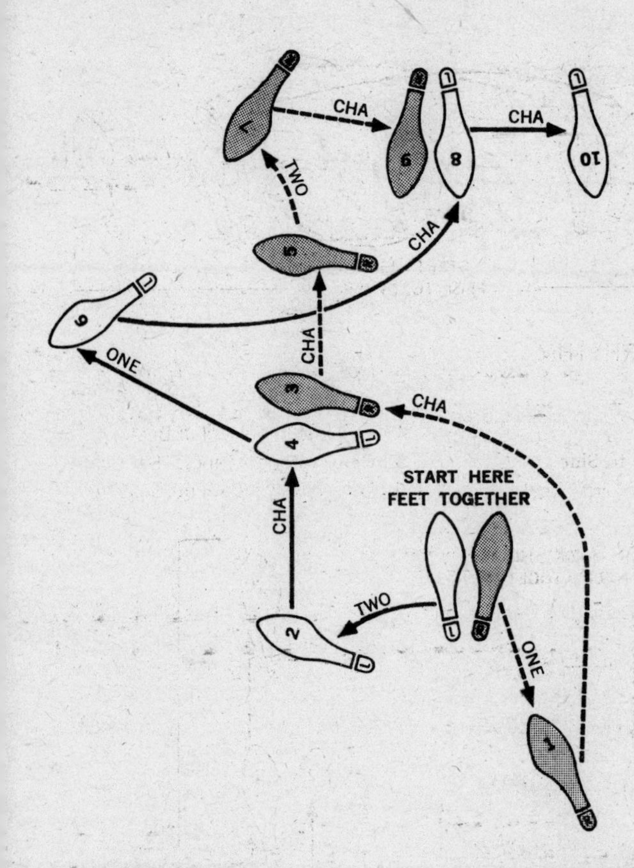

LEFT TURN

Rhythm: One, Two, Cha-Cha-Cha
One, Two, Cha-Cha-Cha

GIRL'S PART:

1. Right foot backward, Full Beat
2. Left foot forward, Full Beat (point toe as shown in diagram)
3. Right foot forward and to side, Half Beat (point toe as shown, so feet are parallel)
4. Close with left foot, Half Beat
5. Right foot to side, Full Beat
6. Left foot forward with toe out, Full Beat (point toe as shown)
7. Right foot backward, Full Beat (point toe as shown)
8. Left foot backward and to side, Half Beat (point toe as shown)
9. Close with right foot, Half Beat
10. Left foot to side, Full Beat

NOTE: See note under man's part.

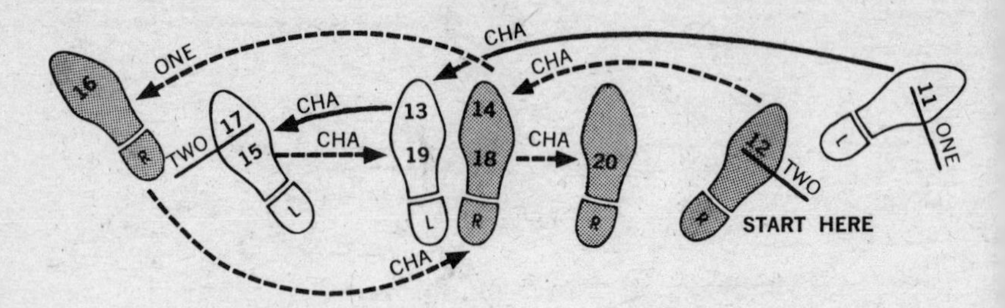

CROSSOVER

Rhythm: One, Two, Cha-Cha-Cha
One, Two, Cha-Cha-Cha

MAN'S PART:

1—10. Same as in Simple Basic Step

11. Left foot forward, Full Beat (cross in front of right foot)

12. Right foot in place, Full Beat

13. Left foot to side, Half Beat (point toe as shown in diagram)

14. Close with right foot, Half Beat

15. Left foot to side, Full Beat (point toe as shown)

16. Right foot forward, Full Beat (cross in front of left foot)

17. Left foot in place, Full Beat

18. Right foot to side, Half Beat (point toe as shown)

19. Close with left foot, Half Beat

20. Right foot to side, Full Beat

NOTE: On the 10th step of the Simple Basic, the man releases his right hand hold, so that both partners are in right open position for steps 11 and 12. The man then changes to left open position on steps 13, 14, and 15, taking the girl's left hand in his right hand. Partners stay in left open position for steps 16 and 17. Return to closed position on steps 18, 19, and 20. (See drawings.)

STEPS 11 and 12 STEPS 16 and 17

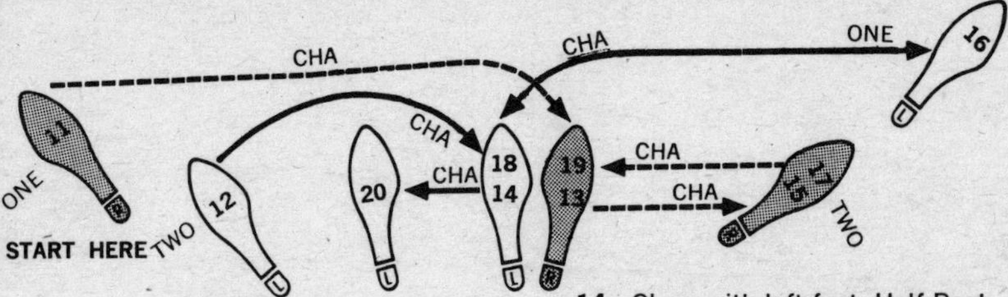

CROSSOVER

Rhythm: One, Two, Cha-Cha-Cha
One, Two, Cha-Cha-Cha

GIRL'S PART:

1.—10. Same as in Simple Basic Step
11. Right foot forward, Full Beat (cross in front of left foot)
12. Left foot in place, Full Beat
13. Right foot to side, Half Beat (point toe as shown in diagram)
14. Close with left foot, Half Beat
15. Right foot to side, Full Beat (point toe as shown)
16. Left foot forward, Full Beat (cross in front of right foot)
17. Right foot in place, Full Beat
18. Left foot to side, Half Beat (point toe as shown)
19. Close with right foot, Half Beat
20. Left foot to side, Full Beat

NOTE: See note under man's part.

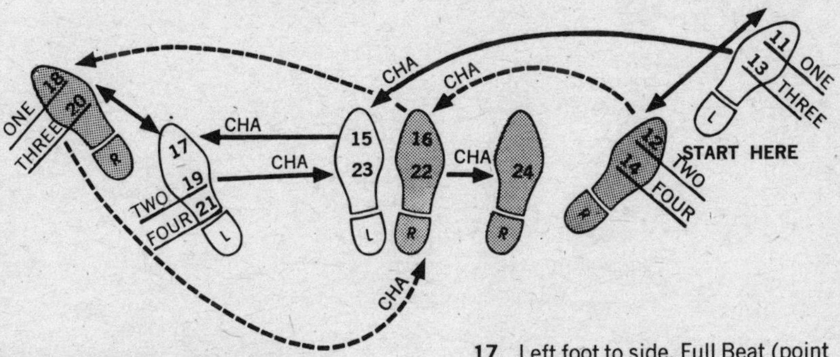

DOUBLE CROSSOVER

Rhythm: One, Two, Three, Four,
Cha-Cha-Cha
One, Two, Three, Four,
Cha-Cha-Cha

MAN'S PART:

1.—10. Same as in Simple Basic Step
11. Left foot forward, Full Beat (Cross in front of right foot)
12. Right foot in place, Full Beat
13. Left foot in place, Full Beat
14. Right foot in place, Full Beat
15. Left foot to side, Half Beat (point toe as shown in diagram)
16. Close with right foot, Half Beat
17. Left foot to side, Full Beat (point toe as shown)
18. Right foot forward, Full Beat (cross in front of left foot)
19. Left foot in place, Full Beat
20. Right foot in place, Full Beat
21. Left foot in place, Full Beat
22. Right foot to side, Half Beat (point toe as shown)
23. Close with left foot, Half Beat
24. Right foot to side, Full Beat

NOTE: See note under Crossover; however, remain in right open position for steps 11, 12, 13, and 14, and in left open position for steps 18, 19, 20, and 21.

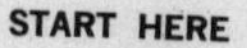

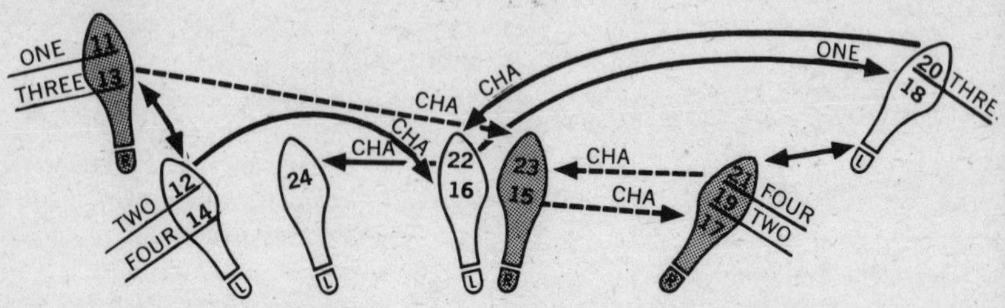

DOUBLE CROSSOVER

Rhythm: One, Two, Three, Four,
Cha-Cha-Cha
One, Two, Three, Four,
Cha-Cha-Cha

GIRL'S PART:

1.—10. Same as in Simple Basic Step
11. Right foot forward, Full Beat (cross in front of left foot)
12. Left foot in place, Full Beat
13. Right foot in place, Full Beat
14. Left foot in place, Full Beat
15. Right foot to side, Half Beat (point toe as shown in diagram)
16. Close with left foot, Half Beat
17. Right foot to side, Full Beat (point toe as shown)
18. Left foot forward, Full Beat (cross in front of right foot)
19. Right foot in place, Full Beat
20. Left foot in place, Full Beat
21. Right foot in place, Full Beat
22. Left foot to side, Half Beat (point toe as shown)
23. Close with right foot, Half Beat
24. Left foot to side, Full Beat

NOTE: See note under man's part.

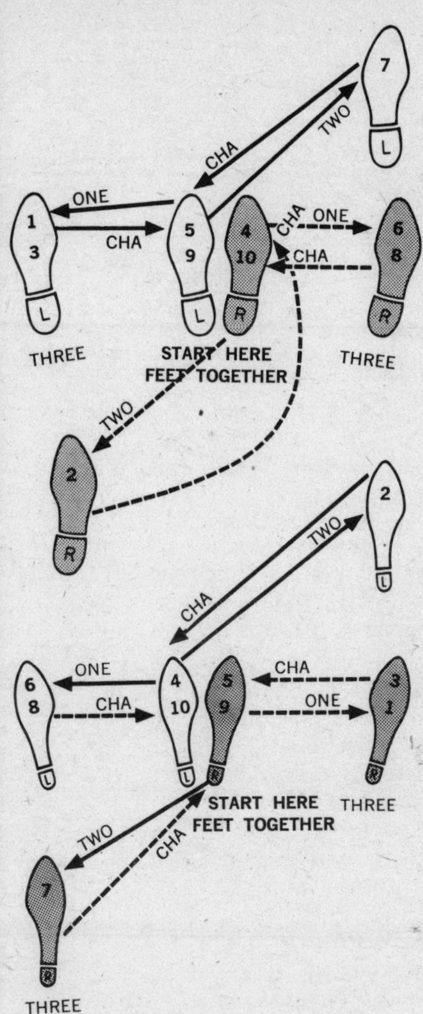

ADVANCED BASIC

Rhythm: One, Two, Three, Cha-Cha
One, Two, Three, Cha-Cha

MAN'S PART:

1. Left foot to side, Full Beat
2. Right foot backward, Full Beat (place toe in line with left heel)
3. Left foot in place, Full Beat
4. Right foot forward and to side, Half Beat
5. Close with left foot, Half Beat
6. Right foot to side, Full Beat
7. Left foot forward, Full Beat (place heel in line with right toe)
8. Right foot in place, Full Beat
9. Left foot backward and to side, Half Beat
10. Close with right foot Half Beat

ADVANCED BASIC

Rhythm: One, Two, Three, Cha-Cha
One, Two, Three, Cha-Cha

GIRL'S PART:

1. Right foot to side, Full Beat
2. Left foot forward, Full Beat (place heel in line with right toe)
3. Right foot in place, Full Beat
4. Left foot backward and to side, Half Beat
5. Close with right foot, Half Beat
6. Left foot to side, Full Beat
7. Right foot backward, Full Beat (place toe in line with left heel)
8. Left foot in place, Full Beat
9. Right foot forward and to side, Half Beat
10. Close with left foot, Half Beat

NOTE: In the Advanced Basic Step, the man begins moving to the side on the first step. He then continues dancing the same pattern as for the Simple Basic, beginning with the backward half first. Other than taking the first step to the side, the footwork for the Advanced Basic is the same as for the Simple Basic. The timing in the Advanced Basic will be altered, due to the first side step, so that each forward and backward break step will be danced on the second beat of the music, rather than the first beat. After you have mastered the Advanced Step, apply the above principles to the other patterns studied.

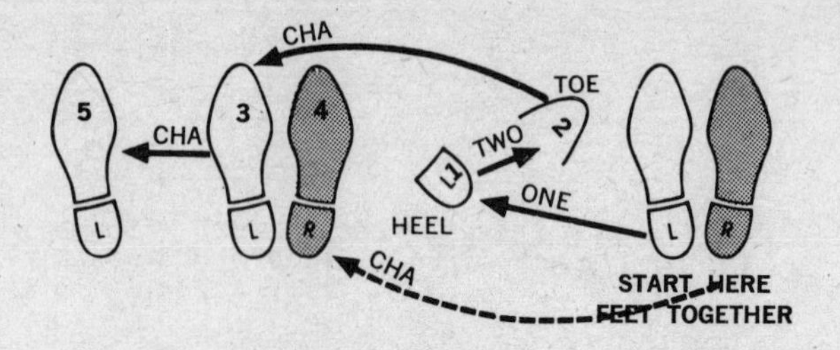

HEEL AND TOE

Rhythm: One, Two, Cha-Cha-Cha
One, Two, Cha-Cha-Cha

MAN'S PART:

1. Left heel to side, Full Beat (keep weight on right leg)
2. Touch left toe to floor, Full Beat (raising heel at same time)
3. Left foot to side, Half Beat
4. Close with right foot, Half Beat
5. Left foot to side, Full Beat
6. Right heel to side, Full Beat (keep weight on left leg)
7. Touch right toe to floor, Full Beat (raising heel at same time)
8. Right foot to side, Half Beat
9. Close with left foot, Half Beat
10. Right foot to side, Full Beat

NOTE: When placing the heel and toe on the floor, do not shift weight to that foot. Maintain all weight on the supporting leg. This step may be danced either in the closed position or the open position holding partner's both hands.

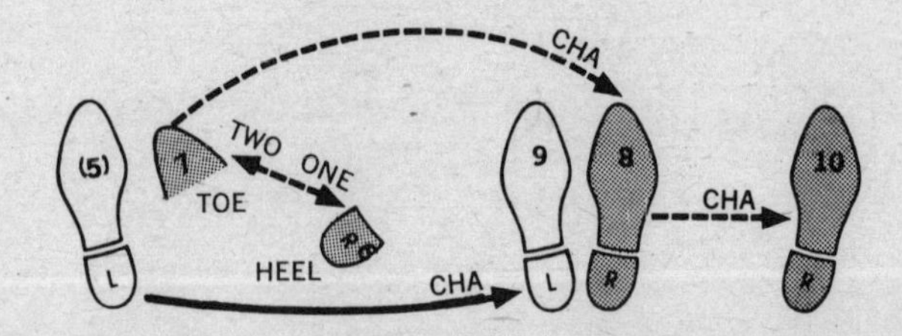

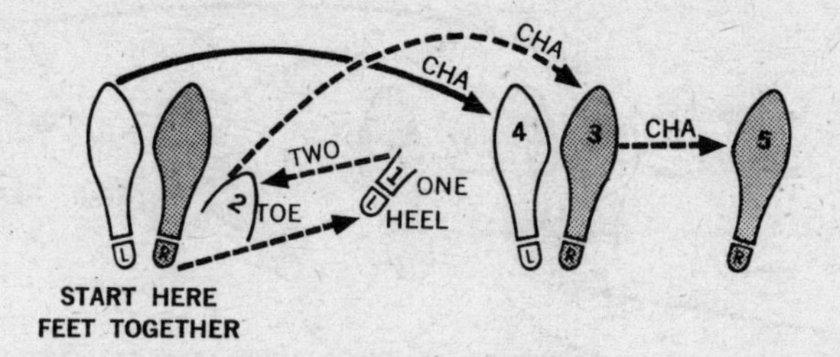

HEEL AND TOE

Rhythm: One, Two, Cha-Cha-Cha
One, Two, Cha-Cha-Cha

GIRL'S PART

1. Right heel to side, Full Beat (keep weight on left leg)
2. Touch right toe to floor, Full Beat (raising heel at same time)
3. Right foot to side, Half Beat
4. Close with left foot, Half Beat
5. Right foot to side, Full Beat
6. Left heel to side, Full Beat (keep weight on right leg)
7. Touch left toe to floor, Full Beat (raising heel at same time)
8. Left foot to side, Half Beat
9. Close with right foot, Half Beat
10. Left foot to side, Full Beat

NOTE: See note under man's part.

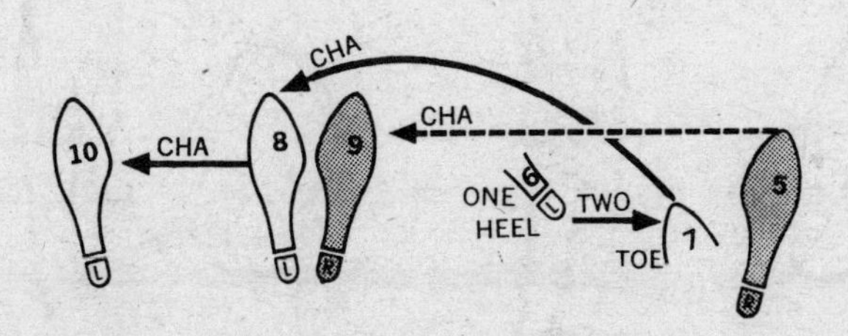

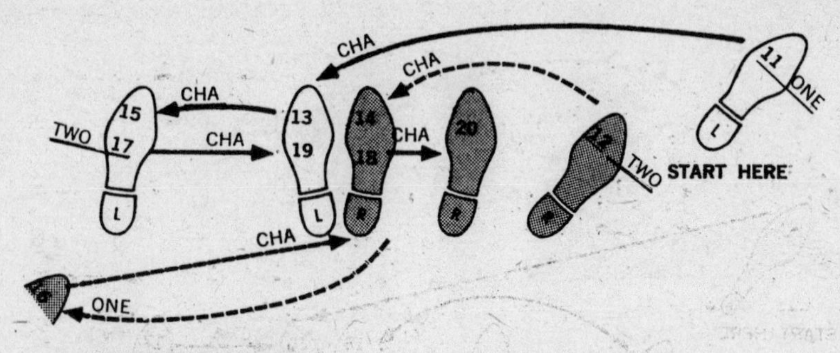

THE BUTTERFLY

Rhythm: One, Two, Cha-Cha-Cha
One, Two, Cha-Cha-Cha

MAN'S PART:

1.—10. Same as Simple Basic Step
11. Left foot forward, Full Beat (cross in front of right foot)
12. Right foot in place, Full Beat
13. Left foot to side, Half Beat (point toe as shown in diagram)
14. Close with right foot, Half Beat
15. Left foot to side, Full Beat
16. Right foot backward, Full Beat (cross behind left foot, putting weight on ball of right foot)
17. Left foot in place, Full Beat
18. Right foot to side, Half Beat (point toe as shown in diagram)
19. Close with left foot, Half Beat
20. Right foot to side, Full Beat

NOTE: The man releases his right hand hold on the 10th step of the Simple Basic. Steps 11 and 12 are danced in right open position. On steps 13 and 14 the man takes partner's both hands and releases his right hand hold once again on step 15. Steps 16 and 17 are danced in right open position. The entire pattern, from step 11 on, may be repeated as many times as desired. The effect achieved is that of the wings of a butterfly opening outward and closing inward. (See drawings.)

STEPS 11 and 12 — STEPS 16 and 17

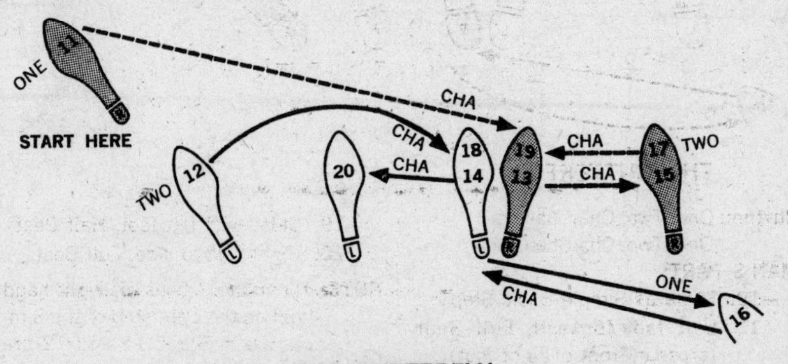

THE BUTTERFLY

Rhythm: One, Two, Cha-Cha-Cha
One, Two, Cha-Cha-Cha

GIRL'S PART:

1.—10. Same as Simple Basic Step

11. Right foot forward, Full Beat (cross in front of left foot)

12. Left foot in place, Full Beat

13. Right foot to side, Half Beat (point toe as shown in diagram)

14. Close with left foot, Half Beat

15. Right foot to side, Full Beat

16. Left foot backward, Full Beat (cross behind right foot, putting weight on ball of left foot)

17. Right foot in place, Full Beat

18. Left foot to side, Half Beat (point toe as shown in diagram)

19. Close with right foot, Half Beat

20. Left foot to side, Full Beat

NOTE: See note under man's part.

THE FLIRT

Rhythm: One, Two, Cha-Cha-Cha
One, Two, Cha-Cha-Cha

MAN'S PART:

1.—10. Same as Progressive Basic Step

11. Left foot forward and pivot to right, Full Beat (pivot halfway to reverse direction)

12. Right foot in place, Full Beat

13. Left foot forward, Half Beat

14. Right foot forward, Half Beat (small step)

15. Left foot forward, Full Beat (small step)

16. Right foot forward and pivot to left, Full Beat (pivot halfway to face starting direction)

17. Left in place, Full Beat

18. Right foot forward, Half Beat

19. Left foot forward, Half Beat (small step)

20. Right foot forward, Full Beat (small step)

NOTE: The Progressive Basic Step is danced in the apart position. Remain in this position, with no hand contact, throughout entire pattern. After the 20th step, continue forward with the left foot into the Simple Basic Step. (See drawings.)

MAN'S STEP 11

MAN'S STEP 12

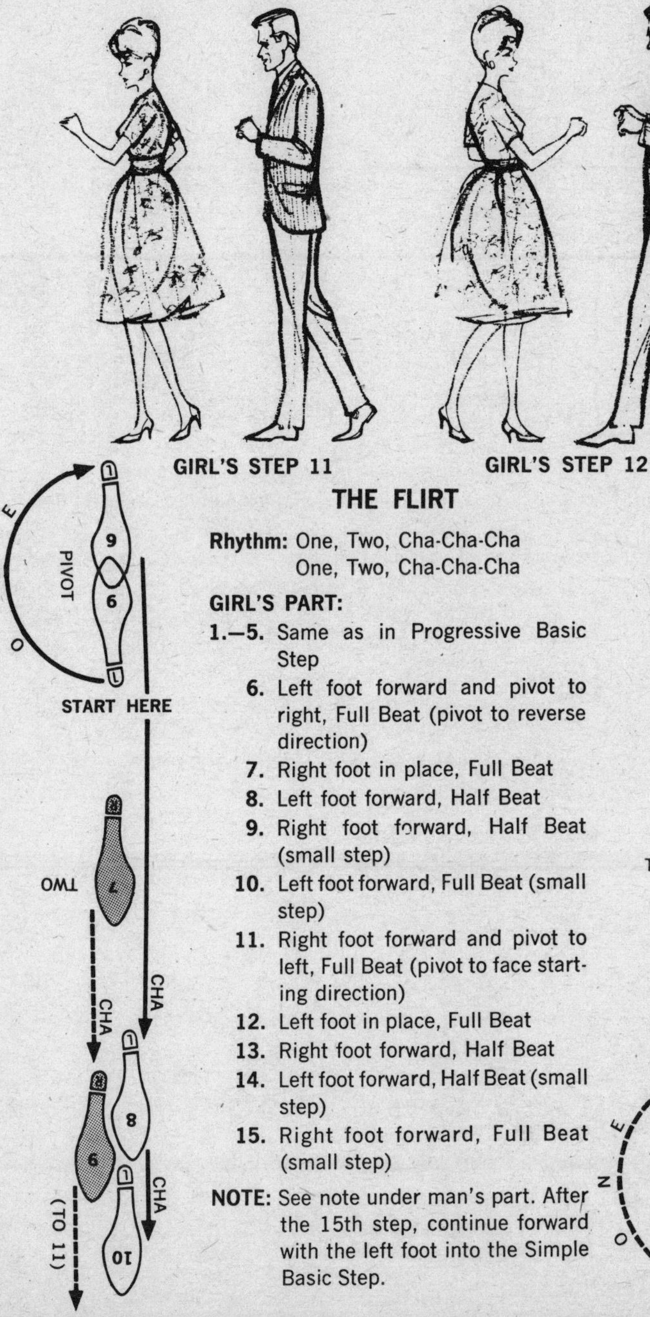

GIRL'S STEP 11

GIRL'S STEP 12

THE FLIRT

Rhythm: One, Two, Cha-Cha-Cha
One, Two, Cha-Cha-Cha

GIRL'S PART:

1.—5. Same as in Progressive Basic Step

6. Left foot forward and pivot to right, Full Beat (pivot to reverse direction)

7. Right foot in place, Full Beat

8. Left foot forward, Half Beat

9. Right foot forward, Half Beat (small step)

10. Left foot forward, Full Beat (small step)

11. Right foot forward and pivot to left, Full Beat (pivot to face starting direction)

12. Left foot in place, Full Beat

13. Right foot forward, Half Beat

14. Left foot forward, Half Beat (small step)

15. Right foot forward, Full Beat (small step)

NOTE: See note under man's part. After the 15th step, continue forward with the left foot into the Simple Basic Step.

Astaire Styling: Cuban Motion

In the Cha Cha Cha, as in the Rumba and Mambo, most of your body motion should be concentrated in your hips. Follow the prescribed method of dancing the Cuban motion as outlined below:

1. Start with your feet together.

2. Keep both legs straight.

3. Bend your left knee forward, still keeping the right leg straight. Your right hip should now be shifted automatically to the right side, without any purposeful effort on your part.

4. Straighten the left leg. You are now in the starting position again—feet together, both legs straight.

5. Bend the right knee forward, still keeping the left leg straight. Your left hip should now be shifted automatically to the left side without any purposeful effort on your part.

6. Straighten the right leg. You are now in the starting position once more—feet together, both legs straight.

No matter in which direction your feet are moving—forward, backward, or sideward—remember this basic rule: When stepping with the left foot, the left knee bends forward; when stepping with the right foot, the right knee bends forward.

You are now ready to apply the Cuban motion to your steps. In the Cha Cha Cha, this motion will not be as smooth as in the Rumba because of the uninhibited effect of the music. The Cha Cha Cha calls for a Cuban hip movement that is almost compulsively timed to the musical tempo and accent. Each shifting of your hips is a distinctly separate action rather than a flowing motion.

Hold yourself tall when you do the Cha Cha Cha. Aside from awkward footwork, perhaps the worst mistake made by unskilled dancers is to bounce up and down like kangaroos. Keep all your steps small and precise, placing more stress on the forward and backward break steps than on the side to side steps.

CHA CHA CHA COMBINATIONS

Pattern	Number of Steps	Rhythm and Count
(A)		
Simple Basic	10	
Heel and Toe	10	All steps: Quick, Quick, Quick And Quick
Simple Basic	10	Count: One, Two, Cha-Cha-Cha
Crossover	10	
(B)		
Progressive Basic	10	All steps: Quick, Quick, Quick And Quick
The Flirt	10	Count: One, Two, Cha-Cha-Cha
Progressive Basic	10	
(C)		
Simple Basic	10	
Double Crossover	14	All steps: Quick, Quick, Quick And Quick
Simple Basic	10	Count: One, Two, Cha-Cha-Cha
The Butterfly	10	
Simple Basic	10	

CHAPTER SEVENTEEN

The Mambo

INTRODUCTION

NO other dance from south of the border has ever attained the instantaneous popularity that the zestful Mambo did when it was first introduced from Latin America. The extent of the Mambo's invasion can be observed in the widespread use of its rhythm by Tin Pan Alley in recent years. Love ballads are being written to a slow Mambo beat; novelty songs to a fast Mambo beat; and Rock 'n' Roll numbers are being tailored to the tempo. The hillbilly idiom has been affected and even classical themes are played to the explosive Mambo beat. Across the nation, dancers who have never progressed beyond the Fox Trot and Waltz are clamoring for Mambo instruction, for here is one of the most abandoned fun-dances of all time.

No doubt many of you will be surprised to learn that the evolution of the Mambo was almost entirely the work of one man: Perez Prado. During the early 1930s, Latin-styled dance bands were coming increasingly often before American audiences, filling the air with Rumbas, Sambas, and Tangos. Then Perez Prado recorded an opus called "Mambo Jambo" and the fun was on.

The Mambo can be danced according to the individual dancer's temperament. Conservative dancers can maintain a closed position, while the more daring can perform breakaway steps and separate frequently from their partners. Facing each other, they can then dance solo, employing an almost endless combination of step patterns.

No matter how fiery your zeal, however, footwork and body motion must be strictly governed by the music. Your knees should be flexed at all times. Neat follow-through is essential when changing from one combination to the next. As in the Rumba, from which it evolved, the Mambo should be danced with most of your body motion concentrated in your hips. Do not exaggerate these body movements; control them, stressing the staccato movements from the waist down and utilizing straight or curved follow-through in the step patterns.

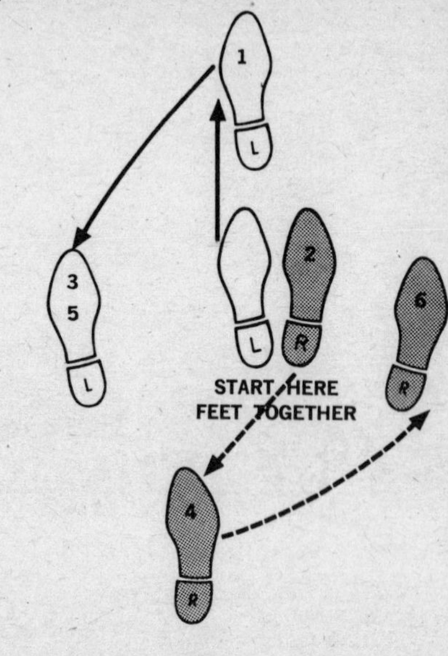

MAMBO BOX STEP

Rhythm: Quick, Quick, Slow
Quick, Quick, Slow

MAN'S PART:

1. Left foot forward, Quick
2. Right foot in place, Quick
3. Left foot backward and to side, Slow
4. Right foot backward, Quick
5. Left foot in place, Quick
6. Right foot forward and to side, Slow

NOTE: The Mambo Box Step is danced in closed position. Take small, precise steps throughout. The ardent Mambo dancer will strive to dance each 1st and 4th step to the second beat of the music, counting in the following manner:

Beat :	1	2	3	4–1	2	3	4–1	
Rhythm:	Hold	Quick	Quick	Slow	Quick	Quick	Slow	etc.
Step :		1	2	3	4	5	6	

If you find this method of counting confusing, count in the way that is easiest for you.

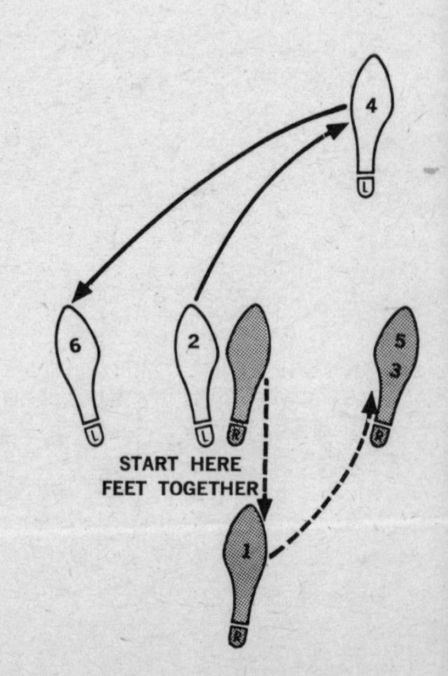

MAMBO BOX STEP

Rhythm: Quick, Quick, Slow
Quick, Quick, Slow

GIRL'S PART:

1. Right foot backward, Quick
2. Left foot in place, Quick
3. Right foot forward and to side, Slow
4. Left foot forward, Quick
5. Right foot in place, Quick
6. Left foot backward and to side, Slow

NOTE: See note under man's part.

PROGRESSIVE BASIC

Rhythm: Quick, Quick, Slow
Quick, Quick, Slow

MAN'S PART:

1. Left foot forward, Quick
2. Right foot in place, Quick
3. Left foot backward, Slow
4. Right foot backward, Quick
5. Left foot in place, Quick
6. Right foot forward, Slow

NOTE: The Progressive Basic is danced in the apart position.

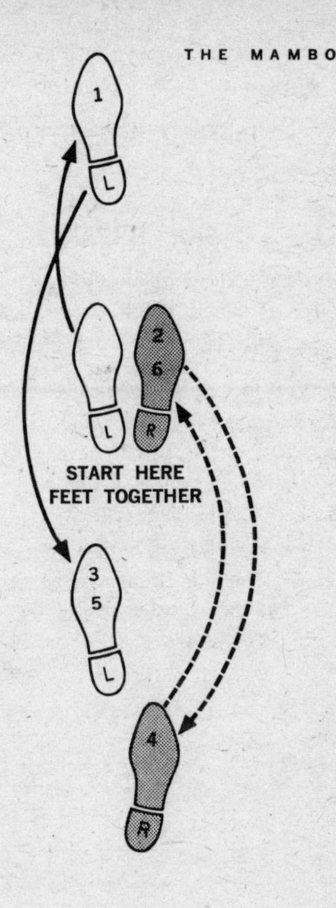

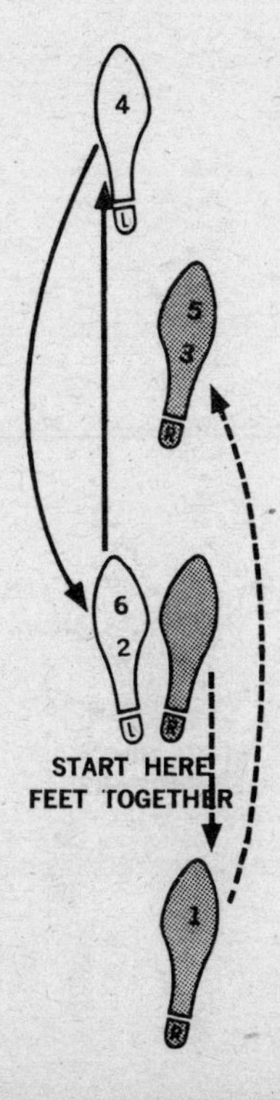

PROGRESSIVE BASIC

Rhythm: Quick, Quick, Slow
Quick, Quick, Slow

GIRL'S PART:

1. Right foot backward, Quick
2. Left foot in place, Quick
3. Right foot forward, Slow
4. Left foot forward, Quick
5. Right foot in place, Quick
6. Left foot backward Slow

NOTE: See note under man's part.

SIDE BREAK

Rhythm: Quick, Quick, Slow
Quick, Quick, Slow

MAN'S PART:

1. Left foot to side, Quick
2. Right foot in place, Quick
3. Close with left foot, Slow
4. Right foot to side, Quick
5. Left foot in place, Quick
6. Close with right foot, Slow

NOTE: The Side Break may be danced in either closed position or apart position.

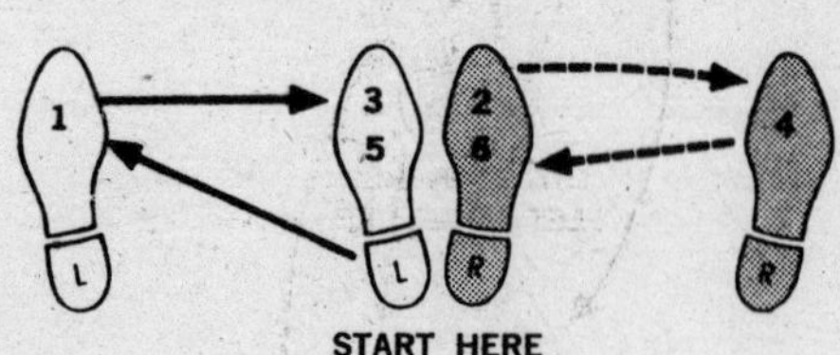

SIDE BREAK

Rhythm: Quick, Quick, Slow
Quick, Quick, Slow

GIRL'S PART:

1. Right foot to side, Quick
2. Left foot in place, Quick
3. Close with right foot, Slow
4. Left foot to side, Quick
5. Right foot in place, Quick
6. Close with left foot, Slow

NOTE: See note under man's part.

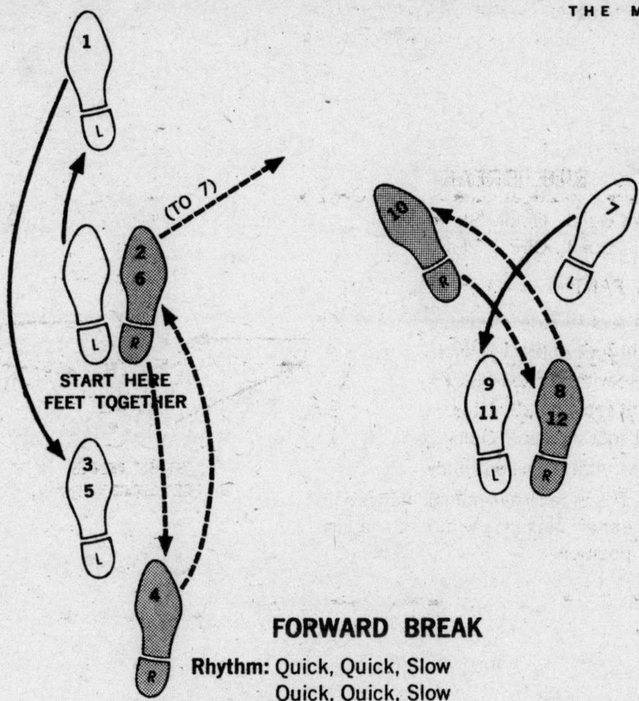

FORWARD BREAK

Rhythm: Quick, Quick, Slow
Quick, Quick, Slow

MAN'S PART:

1. Left foot forward, Quick
2. Right foot in place, Quick
3. Left foot backward, Slow
4. Right foot backward, Quick
5. Left foot in place, Quick
6. Right foot forward, Slow
7. Left foot forward, Quick (place heel directly in line with right toe)
8. Right foot in place, Quick
9. Close with left foot, Slow
10. Right foot forward, Quick (place heel directly in line with left toe)
11. Left foot in place, Quick
12. Close with right foot, Slow

NOTE: The first 6 steps of the forward Break are the Progressive Basic. Partners are in the apart dance position, with no hand contact. Steps 7 through 12 may be repeated as many times as desired.

FORWARD BREAK

Rhythm: Quick, Quick, Slow
Quick, Quick, Slow

GIRL'S PART:

1. Right foot backward, Quick
2. Left foot in place, Quick
3. Right foot forward, Slow
4. Left foot forward, Quick (place heel directly in line with right toe)
5. Right foot in place, Quick
6. Close left foot, Slow
7. Right foot forward, Quick (place heel directly in line with left toe)
8. Left foot in place, Quick
9. Close with right foot, Slow
10. Left foot forward, Quick (place heel directly in line with right toe)
11. Right foot in place, Quick
12. Close with left foot, Slow

NOTE: As the man does the Forward Break, the girl also does the forward Break. The first 3 steps of this pattern are done the same as the Progressive Basic. Partners are in the apart dance position, with no hand contact.

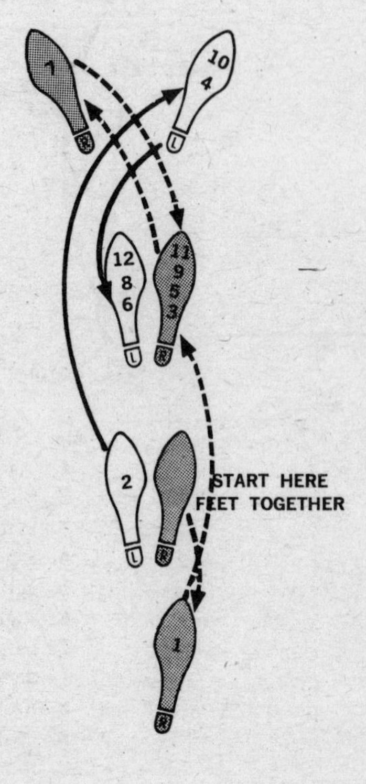

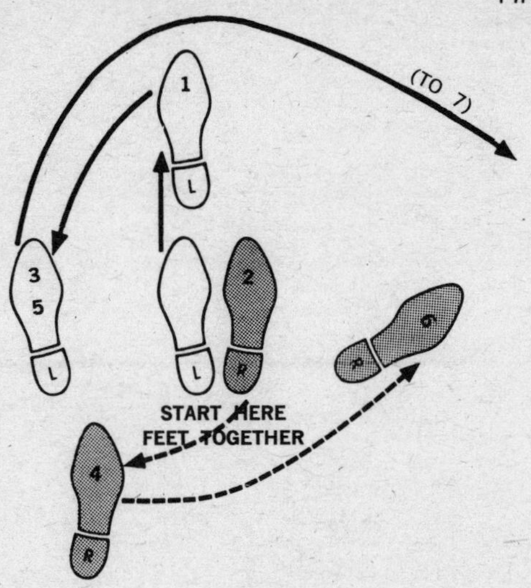

CROSSOVER

Rhythm: Quick, Quick, Slow
Quick, Quick, Slow

MAN'S PART:

1. Left foot forward, Quick
2. Right foot in place, Quick
3. Left foot backward and to side, Slow
4. Right foot backward, Quick
5. Left foot in place, Quick
6. Right foot forward, Slow (point toe as shown in diagram)
7. Left foot forward, Quick (cross foot in front of right foot with left heel directly in line with right toe)
8. Right foot in place, Quick
9. Left foot to side, Slow (point toe as shown in diagram)
10. Right foot forward, Quick (cross foot in front of left foot with right heel directly in line with left toe)
11. Left foot in place, Quick
12. Right foot to side, Slow (point toe as shown)

NOTE: On the 6th step the man releases his right hand hold, turning to his right at the same time. Steps 7 and 8 are in the right open position. Steps 9, 10, and 11 are in the left open position. Refer to Chapter 10, "The Dance Positions."

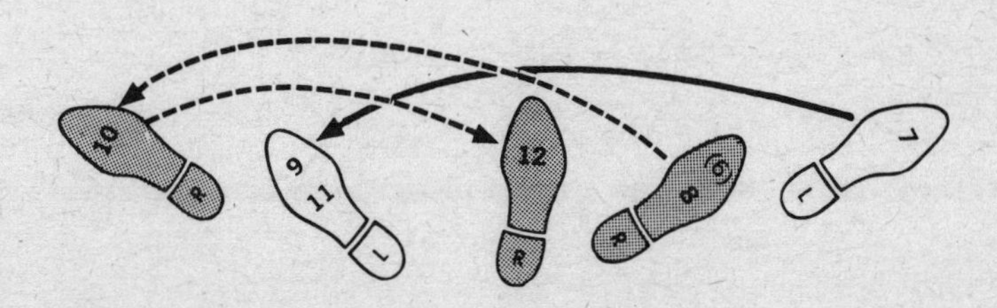

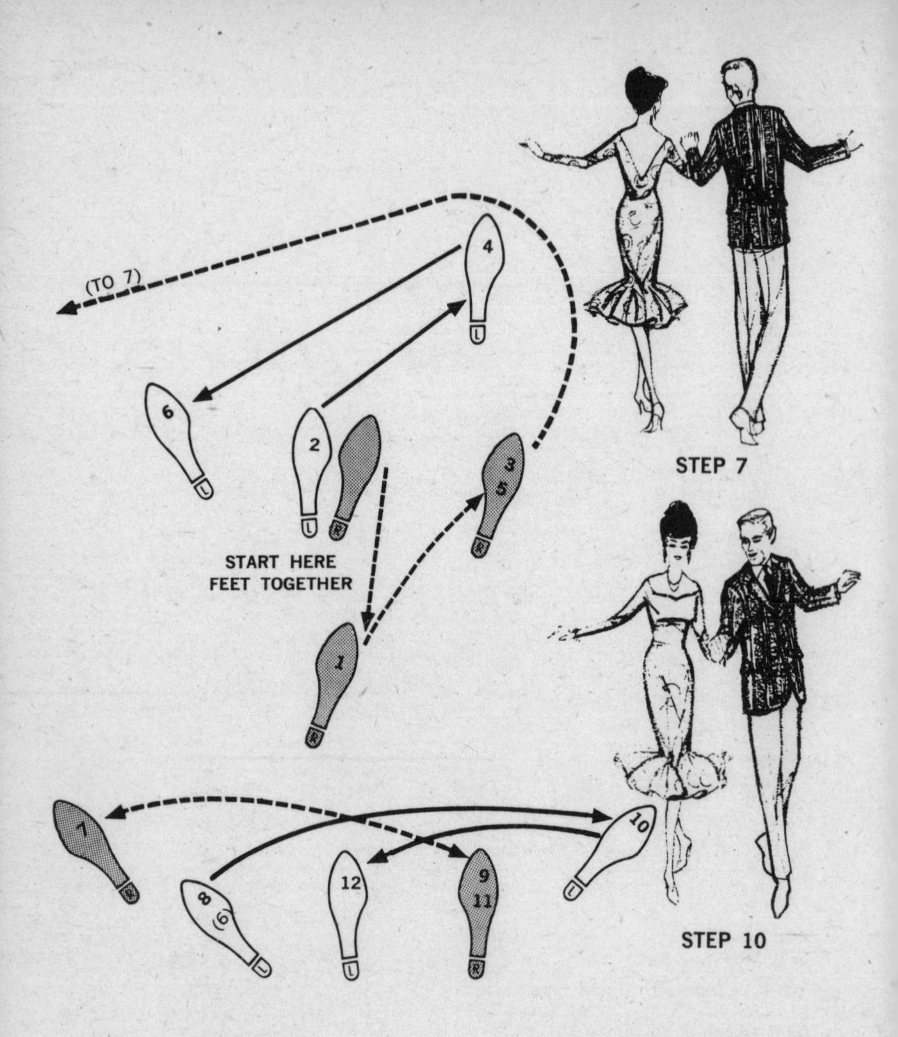

CROSSOVER

Rhythm: Quick, Quick, Slow
Quick, Quick, Slow

GIRL'S PART:

1. Right foot backward, Quick
2. Left foot in place, Quick
3. Right foot forward and to side, Slow
4. Left foot forward, Quick
5. Right foot in place, Quick
6. Left foot forward, Slow (point toe as shown in diagram)
7. Right foot forward, Quick (cross in front of left foot, placing heel directly in line with left toe)
8. Left foot in place, Quick
9. Right foot to side, Slow (point toe as shown in diagram)
10. Left foot forward, Quick (cross in front of right foot, placing heel directly in line with right toe)
11. Right foot in place, Quick
12. Left foot to side, Slow (point toe as shown)

NOTE: See note under man's part.

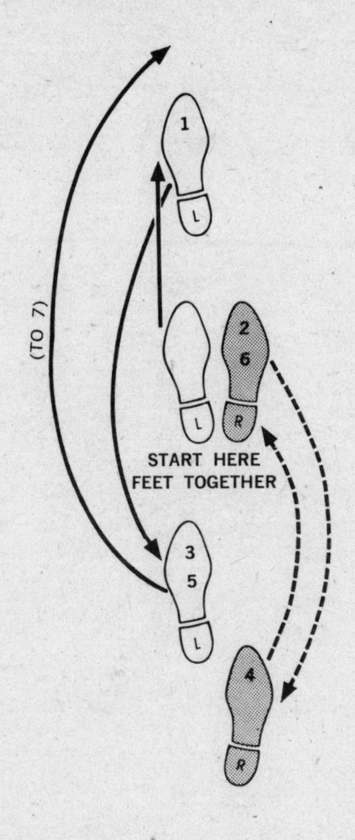

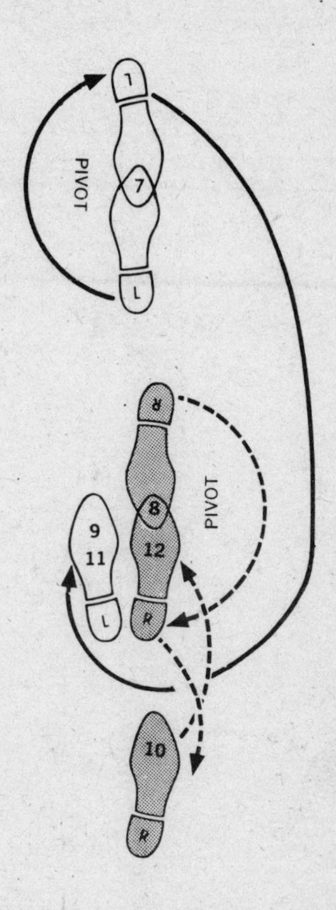

OPEN CHASE—FULL TURN

Rhythm: Quick, Quick, Slow
Quick, Quick, Slow

MAN'S PART:

1. Left foot forward, Quick
2. Right foot in place, Quick
3. Left foot backward, Slow
4. Right foot backward, Quick
5. Left foot in place, Quick
6. Right foot forward, Slow
7. Left foot forward and pivot to right, Quick (place foot directly in front of right foot, pivoting as it touches floor to face opposite direction)
8. Right foot forward and pivot to right, Quick (continue pivoting on ball of right foot until facing original direction; start bringing your left foot around for next step)
9. Close with left foot, Slow (feet are together, pointed in original direction; full turn is completed)
10. Right foot backward, Quick
11. Left foot in place, Quick
12. Close with right foot, Slow

NOTE: The first 6 steps are the Progressive Basic Step, danced in the apart position. There is no hand contact during the execution of this pattern.

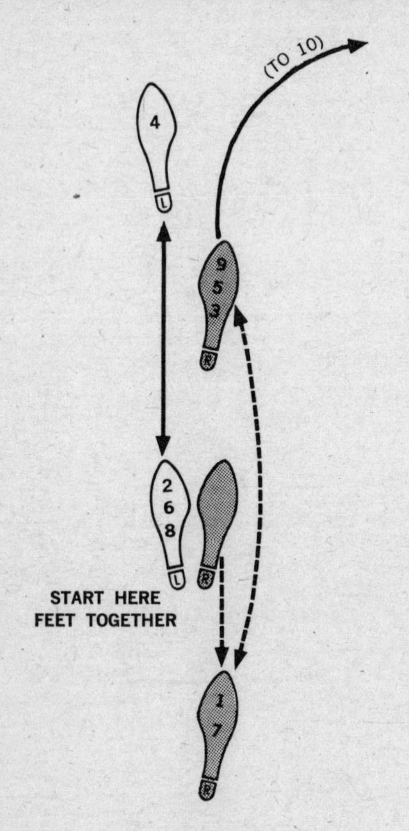

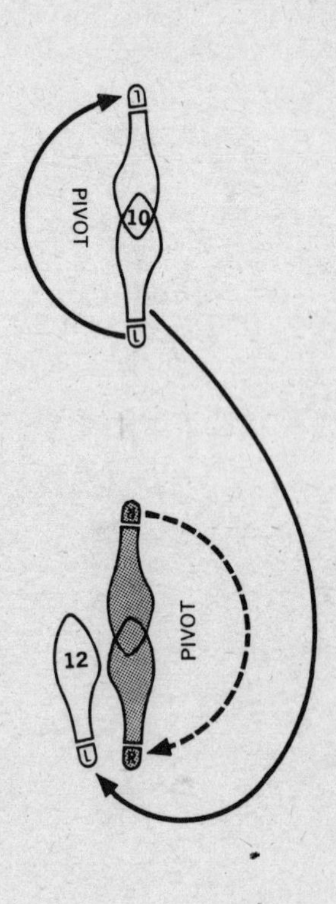

OPEN CHASE—FULL TURN

Rhythm: Quick, Quick, Slow
Quick, Quick, Slow

GIRL'S PART:

1. Right foot backward, Quick
2. Left foot in place, Quick
3. Right foot forward, Slow
4. Left foot forward, Quick
5. Right foot in place, Quick
6. Left foot backward, Slow
7. Right foot backward, Quick
8. Left foot in place, Quick
9. Right foot forward, Slow
10. Left foot forward and pivot to right, Quick (place foot directly in front of right foot, pivoting as it touches floor to face opposite direction)
11. Right foot forward and pivot to right, Quick (continue to pivot on right foot until facing original direction, at the same time bringing your left leg around for final step)
12. Close with left foot, Slow (full turn is completed)

NOTE: The first 9 steps are the Progressive Basic Step, danced in the apart position. The man executes his turn on the 7th, 8th, and 9th steps; the girl on the 10th, 11th, and 12th steps.

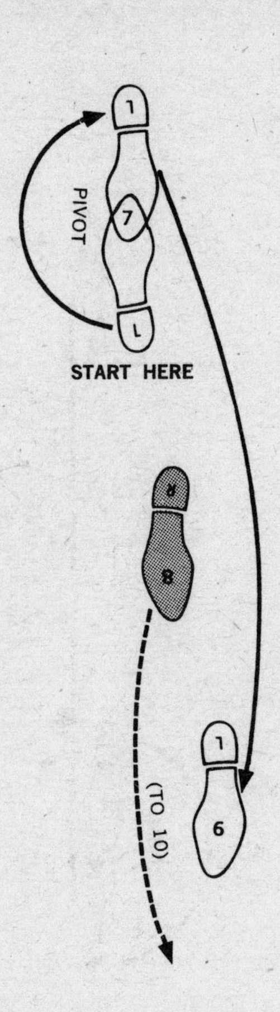

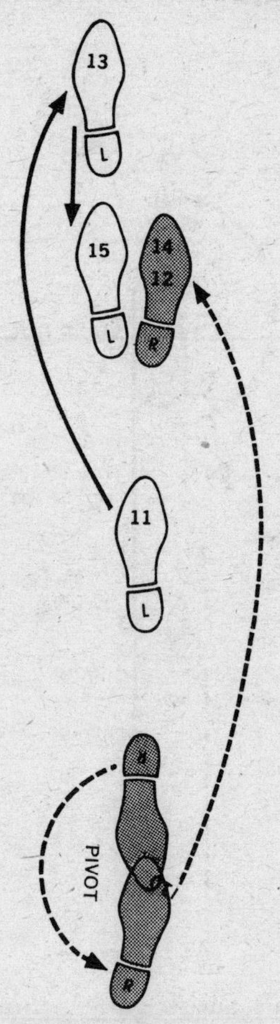

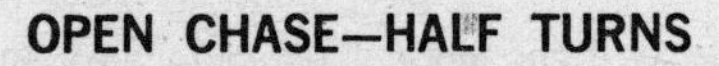

OPEN CHASE—HALF TURNS

Rhythm: Quick, Quick, Slow
Quick, Quick, Slow

MAN'S PART:

1.—6. Same as in Open Chase—Full Turn

7. Left foot forward and pivot to right, Quick (face opposite direction)

8. Right foot forward, Quick

9. Left foot forward, Slow

10. Right foot forward and pivot to left, Quick (same as foregoing pivot)

11. Left foot forward, Quick

12. Right foot forward, Slow

13. Left foot forward, Quick

14. Right foot in place, Quick

15. Close with left foot, Slow

NOTE: Begin the same as in Open Chase —Full Turn, in the apart position. After the 15th step, continue dancing the Progressive Basic Step, waiting for the girl to complete her turn, then return to the closed position.

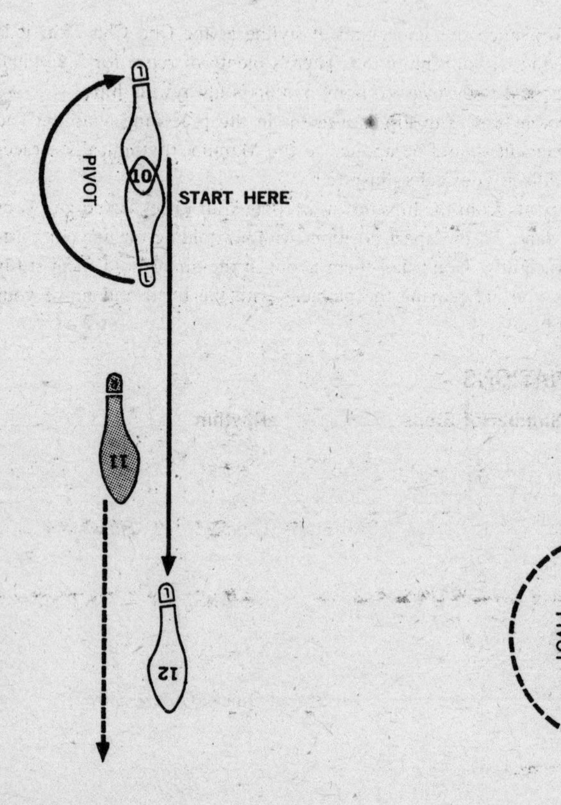

OPEN CHASE—HALF TURNS

Rhythm: Quick, Quick, Slow
Quick, Quick, Slow

GIRL'S PART:

1.—9. Same as in Open Chase—Full Turn

10. Left foot forward and pivot to right, Quick (face in opposite direction)

11. Right foot forward, Quick

12. Left foot forward, Slow

13. Right foot forward and pivot to left, Quick (same as foregoing pivot)

14. Left foot forward, Quick

15. Right foot forward, Slow

NOTE: The girl begins her turn on the 10th step, after the man makes his turn. After the 15th step, she continues forward with the left foot and dances the Progressive Basic Step.

Astaire Styling: The Cuban Motion

The Mambo calls for much the same kind of styling as the Cha Cha Cha; it is danced with freedom and without inhibition. There's plenty of room for individual interpretation, but the focal point of good body motion is always the hips.

Reread the description of Cuban hip movement in the preceding chapter. The same side-to-side movement should be applied to the Mambo, rhythmically, gracefully, and enthusiastically if you feel so inspired.

Project your movements from the hips down, keeping your knees flexed and your body relaxed. If you dance in the apart position, without holding on to your partner, use your arms gracefully. Don't flail them about in the air or hold them stiffly at your side. Imagine you are playing the maracas with the band and move your arms and hands accordingly.

MAMBO COMBINATIONS

Pattern	Number of Steps	Rhythm
(A)		
Box Step	6	
Side Break	6	
Box Step	6	All Steps: Quick, Quick, Slow
Crossover	6	
Mambo Box Step	6	
(B)		
Progressive Basic	6	
Open Chase—Half Turns	6	All Steps: Quick, Quick, Slow
Progressive Basic	6	
Open Chase—Full Turn	6	
Progressive Basic	6	
(C)		
Progressive Basic	6	
Forward Break	12	All Steps: Quick, Quick, Slow
Progressive Basic	6	

CHAPTER EIGHTEEN

The Lindy Swing

INTRODUCTION

THE Lindy, or Jitterbug, originated in the American Southland, along with most other jazz forms. It is related to such memorable dances as the Charleston, Black Bottom, and Shag. In the early 1940s, the best features of all these dances were consolidated into the Lindy Hop, which is now called the Lindy.

Initially, the Lindy was performed as a modified box step with a distinct shuffling movement. This shuffle is what makes the faster tempo of the Lindy into the Single Lindy. The Triple Lindy, which is more popular than the Single Lindy, is danced to the slower tempos. There is no question that the Lindy is here to stay; in all sections of the country you will find people adding their own interpretations and changes of style. All dances, in order to survive, must have a firm basic pattern so that ad-libbing can be enjoyed. The Lindy has this attribute. Furthermore, the Lindy can be danced expertly in a relatively small area.

The main points to watch are to keep your body relaxed and your knees flexed. The closed dance position in the Lindy is actually a semi-left open position, with the man's right arm reaching farther around the girl's back. The most characteristic movements of the dance are a slight bounce with the knees and a swaying of the upper part of the body. The syncopated beat of the music imparts exuberance and vigor to the dance. You may find yourself letting go of your inhibitions on the dance floor and doing whatever steps the music inspires you to do!

At the outset, however, confine yourself to the step patterns taught in this book. Do them to slow swing music at first, then gradually increase the tempo. You'll find, however, that you do not necessarily have to dance fast to have fun.

BASIC SWING

Rhythm: Slow, Slow, Quick, Quick
(Single Rhythm)

MAN'S PART:

1. Left foot to side, Slow
2. Right foot to right side, Slow
3. Left foot backward, Quick (place toe behind right heel, putting weight on ball of left foot)
4. Right foot in place, Quick

NOTE: Stand in a position halfway between the closed and left open positions. Hold the left arm down, close to the body rather than upward as in the normal Ballroom Hold. This positioning of the body and hand hold has become a popular trademark of the Lindy Swing. In the following patterns, this position will be referred to as closed position. (See drawing.)

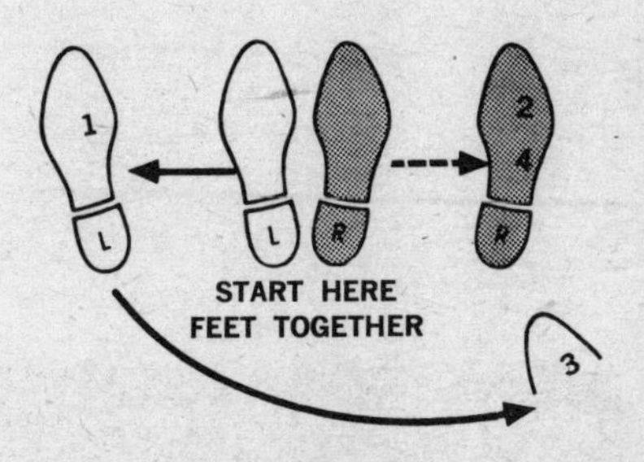

BASIC SWING

Rhythm: Slow, Slow, Quick, Quick
(Single Rhythm)

GIRL'S PART:

1. Right foot to side, Slow
2. Left foot to left side, Slow
3. Right foot backward, Quick (place toe behind left heel, putting weight on ball of right foot)
4. Left foot in place, Quick

NOTE: See note under man's part.

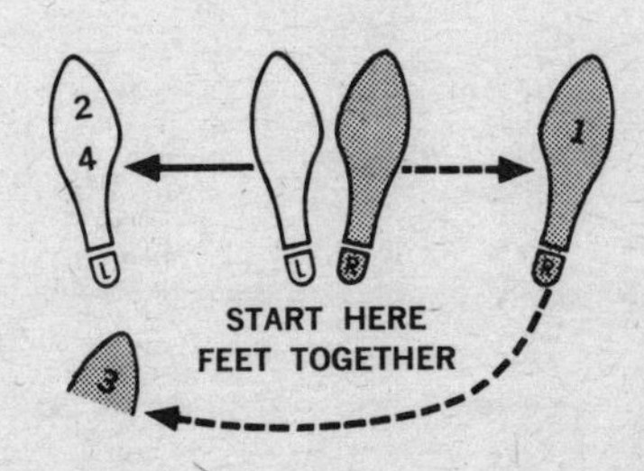

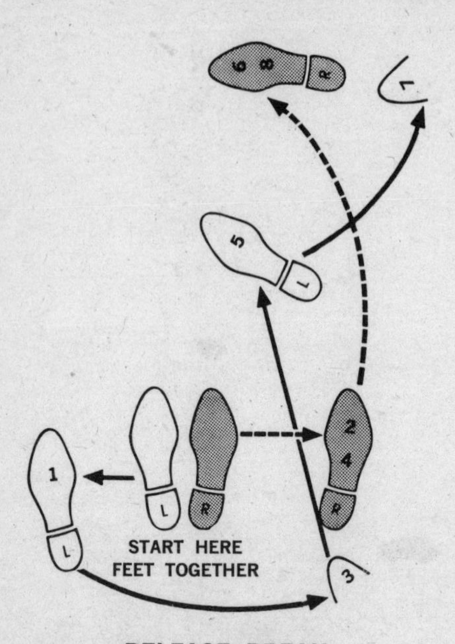

RELEASE BREAK

Rhythm: Slow, Slow, Quick, Quick
Slow, Slow, Quick, Quick

MAN'S PART:

1. Left foot to side, Slow
2. Right foot to right side, Slow
3. Left foot backward, Quick (place toe behind right heel, putting weight on ball of left foot)
4. Right foot in place, Quick
5. Left foot forward, Slow (point toe as shown in diagram)
6. Right foot forward and to side, Slow (point toe as shown)
7. Left foot backward, Quick (place toe behind right heel, putting weight on ball of left foot)
8. Right foot in place, Quick

NOTE: As the man points his toe out on the 5th step (forward), he turns his body slightly to the left, at the same time releasing his right hand hold, so that the 6th, 7th, and 8th steps are danced in the open position.

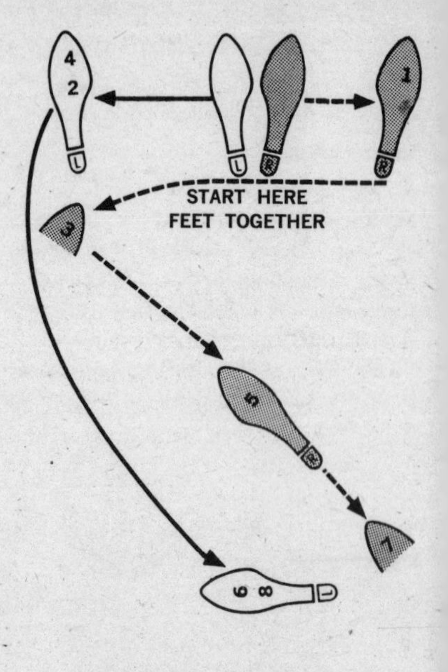

RELEASE BREAK

Rhythm: Slow, Slow, Quick, Quick
Slow, Slow, Quick, Quick

GIRL'S PART:

1. Right foot to side, Slow
2. Left foot to left side, Slow
3. Right foot backward, Quick (place toe behind left heel, putting weight on ball of right foot)
4. Left foot in place, Quick
5. Right foot backward, Slow (point toe as shown in diagram)
6. Left foot backward and to side, Slow (point toe as shown)
7. Right foot backward, Quick (place toe behind left heel, putting weight on ball of right foot)
8. Left foot in place, Quick

NOTE: On the 5th step, the man leads the girl to break away from the closed position. When he leads this step, the girl removes her left hand from behind his right shoulder, and continues dancing her pattern in the open position.

BRIDGE BREAK

Rhythm: Slow, Slow, Quick, Quick
Slow, Slow, Quick, Quick

MAN'S PART:

The man dances the Basic Swing Step, at the same time leading his partner to turn under his left arm. He leads her to turn first to her right and then to her left. Study the drawings on this page, then practice the Bridge Break with an imaginary partner.

GIRL'S STEP 1

GIRL'S STEP 2

GIRL'S STEPS 3 and 4

GIRL'S STEP 5

GIRL'S STEPS 6, 7, 8

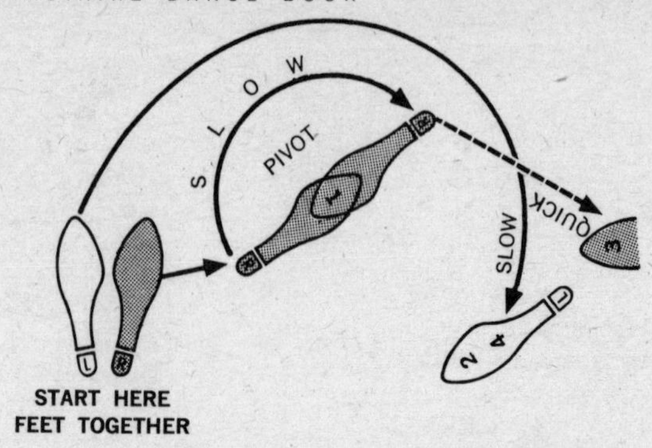

BRIDGE BREAK

Rhythm: Slow, Slow, Quick, Quick

GIRL'S PART: Right Turn

1. Right foot to side and pivot to right, Slow (point toe as shown in diagram)
2. Left foot to side, Slow (while pivoting on right foot, swing left foot around and behind right foot to next position
3. Right foot backward, Quick (place toe behind left heel, putting weight on ball of right foot)
4. Left foot in place, Quick

GIRL'S PART: Left Turn

5. Right foot forward and pivot to left, Slow (reverse direction)
6. Left foot backward and to side, Slow (you will find it necessary to start releasing left foot midway through right foot pivot)
7. Right foot backward, Quick (place toe behind left heel, putting weight on ball of right foot)
8. Left foot in place, Quick

NOTE: The girl executes the Bridge Break, turning right and then left under the man's arm as he does the Basic Swing Step. Study directions and drawings on facing page.

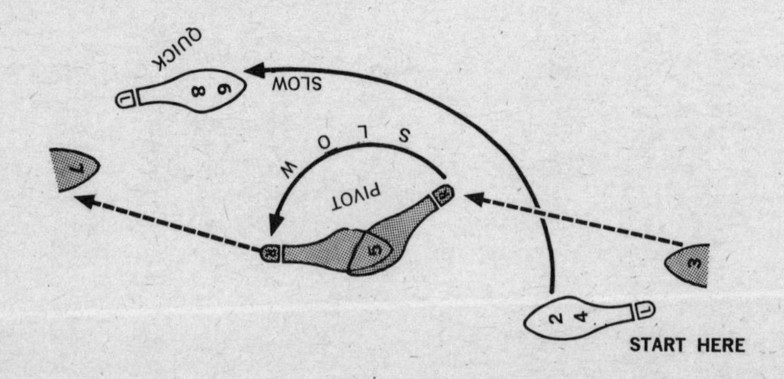

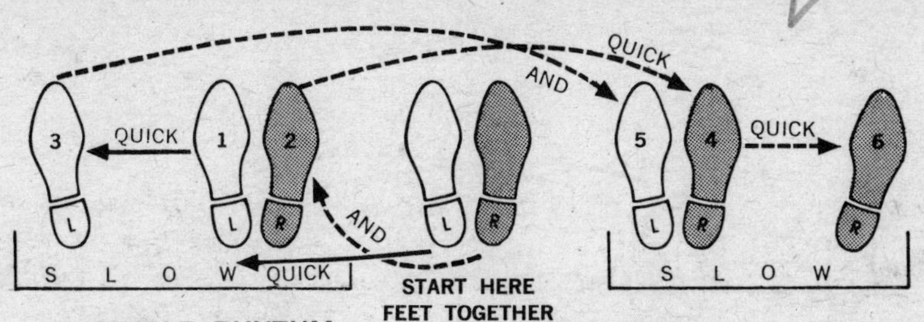

TRIPLE RHYTHM

Rhythm: Quick And Quick
Quick And Quick

MAN'S PART: Side to Side

1. Left foot to side, Half Beat
2. Close with right foot, Half Beat
3. Left foot to side, Full Beat
4. Right foot to right side, Half Beat
5. Close with left foot, Half Beat
6. Right foot to side, Full Beat

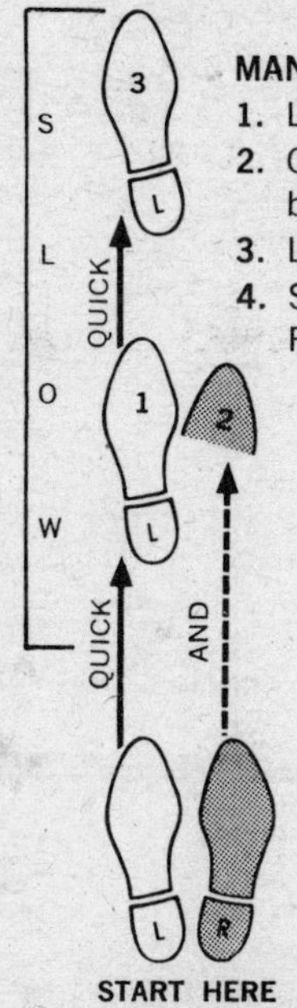

MAN'S PART: Forward

1. Left foot forward, Half Beat
2. Close with right foot, Half Beat (on ball of foot)
3. Left foot forward, Full Beat
4. Same steps as 1, 2, 3 of girl's part for Forward Triple with right foot

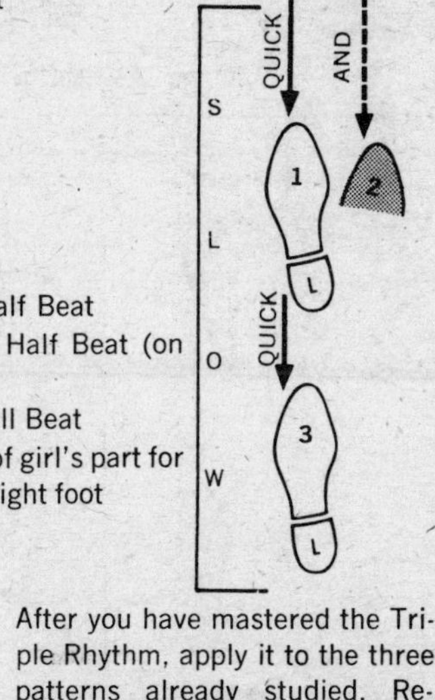

MAN'S PART: Backward

1. Left foot backward, Half Beat
2. Close with right foot, Half Beat (on ball of foot)
3. Left foot backward, Full Beat
4. Same steps as 1, 2, 3 of girl's part for Backward Triple with right foot

NOTE: Each three-step sequence is taken to two beats of music. In the Triple Rhythm, only the slow step is altered; the quick steps remain the same as in the Basic Swing. Remember, Triple Rhythm is used only to the slow tempo Lindy music. If you were to dance Triple Rhythm to fast music, you would appear to be struggling with the dance rather than enjoying it.

After you have mastered the Triple Rhythm, apply it to the three patterns already studied. Remember, alter only the slow steps to Triple Rhythm and dance the quick steps as you would for the Basic Swing. Try counting aloud in the following manner: Quick And Quick—Quick and Quick—Quick-Quick, or 1 and 2—3 and 4—Quick-Quick.

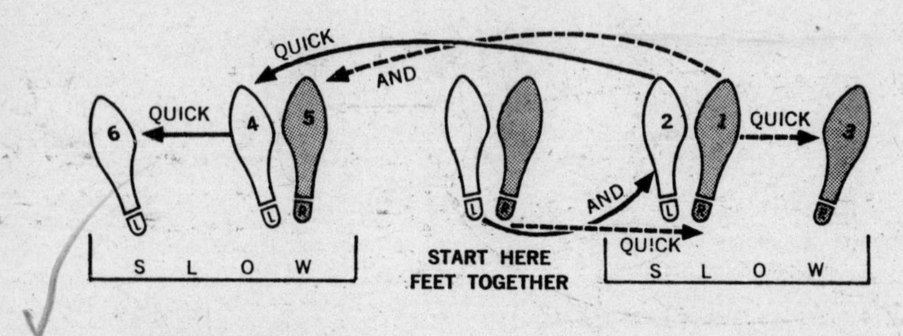

TRIPLE RHYTHM

Rhythm: Quick And Quick
Quick And Quick

GIRL'S PART: Side to Side

1. Right foot to side, Half Beat
2. Close with left foot, Half Beat
3. Right foot to side, Full Beat
4. Left foot to side, Half Beat
5. Close with right foot, Half Beat
6. Left foot to side, Full Beat

START HERE
FEET TOGETHER
AND
QUICK
2
1
QUICK
3
S L O W

GIRL'S PART: Backward

1. Right foot backward, Half Beat
2. Close with left foot, Half Beat
3. Right foot backward, Full Beat
4. Same steps as 1, 2, 3 of man's part for Backward Triple with left foot.

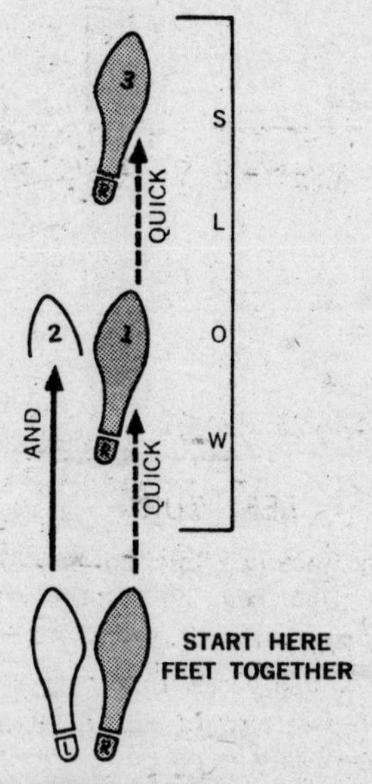

GIRL'S PART: Forward

1. Right foot forward, Half Beat
2. Close with left foot, Half Beat
3. Right foot forward, Half Beat
4. Same steps as 1, 2, 3 of man's part for Forward Triple with left foot.

NOTE: See note under man's part.

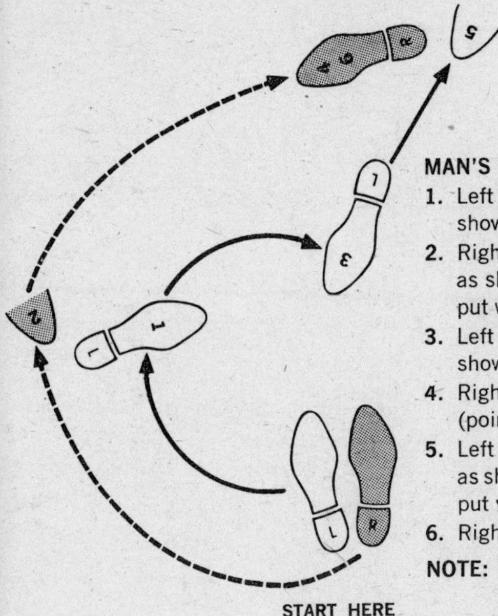

BASIC TURN

Rhythm: Slow, Quick, Quick
Slow, Quick, Quick

MAN'S PART:

1. Left foot to side, Slow (point toe as shown in diagram)
2. Right foot backward, Quick (point toe as shown, placing it behind left heel; put weight on ball of right foot)
3. Left foot to side, Quick (point toe as shown)
4. Right foot backward and to side, Slow (point toe as shown)
5. Left foot backward, Quick (point toe as shown, putting it behind right heel; put weight on ball of left foot)
6. Right foot in place, Quick

NOTE: Turn halfway to the right on steps 1, 2, and 3. Steps 4, 5, and 6 are the same as in the Basic Swing Step. When leading your partner, make sure Step 1 is taken around in front of her so that her first step is placed in between your feet.

BASIC TURN

Rhythm: Slow, Quick, Quick
Slow, Quick, Quick

GIRL'S PART:

1. Right foot forward, Slow (point toe as shown in diagram)
2. Left foot forward and around, Quick (when turning on right foot, bring left foot around to next position on the floor)
3. Right foot forward, Quick (point toe as shown)
4. Left foot to side, Slow (point toe as shown)
5. Right foot backward, Quick (place toe behind left heel, putting weight on ball of right foot)
6. Left foot in place, Quick

NOTE: The first step is taken in between the man's feet. Turn to the right between steps 1 and 3. Steps 4, 5, and 6 are the same as in the Basic Swing Step.

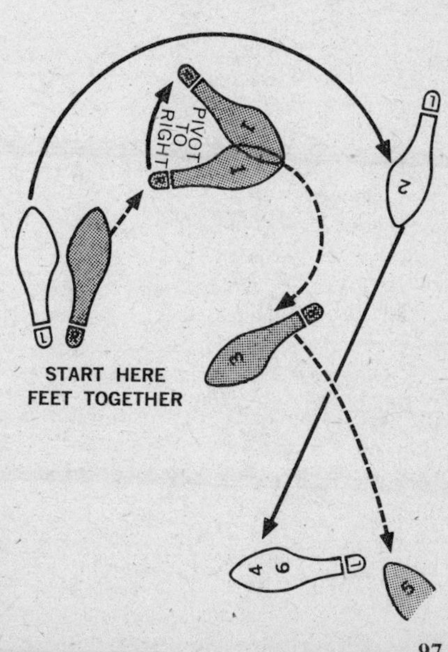

BASIC BREAKAWAY

Rhythm: Slow, Quick, Quick
Slow, Quick, Quick

MAN'S PART:

1. Left foot to side, Slow (point toe as shown in diagram)
2. Right foot backward, Quick (point toe as shown, placing it behind left heel; put weight on ball of right foot)
3. Left foot to side, Quick (point toe as shown)
4. Right foot backward diagonal, Slow (point toe as shown)
5. Left foot backward, Quick (place toe alongside right heel, putting weight on ball of left foot)
6. Right foot in place, Quick

NOTE: Steps 1, 2, and 3 are the same as in the Basic Turn—turning halfway to right. On step 4, the man releases his right hand hold and steps backward into the open position, holding his partner with his left hand. Remain in open position for steps 4, 5, and 6.

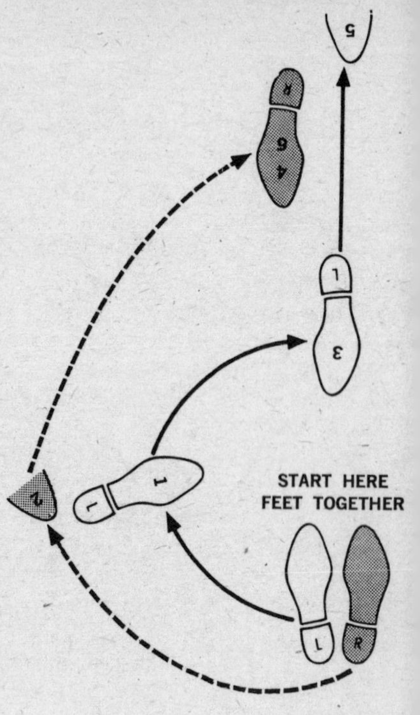

BASIC BREAKAWAY

Rhythm: Slow, Quick, Quick
Slow, Quick, Quick

GIRL'S PART:

1. Right foot forward, Slow (point toe as shown in diagram)
2. Left foot forward and around, Quick (point toe as shown)
3. Right foot forward, Quick (point toe as shown)
4. Left foot forward and to side, Slow (pivot as necessary on right foot in order to bring left foot around; point left toe as shown)
5. Right foot backward, Quick (place toe alongside left heel, putting weight on ball of right foot)
6. Left foot in place, Quick

NOTE: Steps 1, 2, and 3 are the same as the Basic Turn. The man will release his right hand hold on step 4. Continue dancing steps 4, 5, and 6 the same as in steps 6, 7, and 8 of the Release Break.

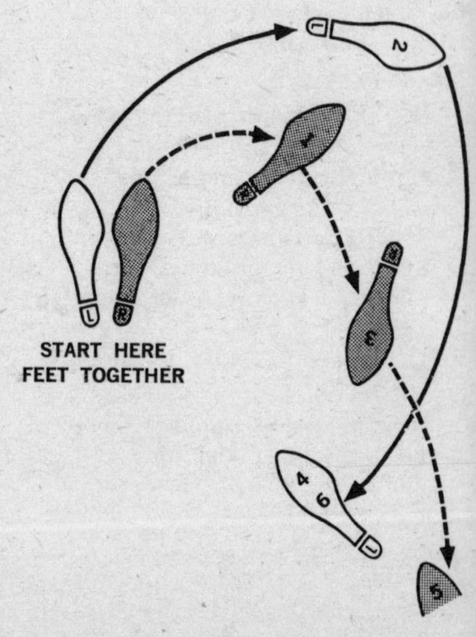

Astaire Styling: The Lindy Swing

The foremost requirement for dancing the Lindy is relaxation and flexibility in the knees. You should feel free to move in any and all directions: sideways, forward, backward. By picking up your feet and placing them on the floor in the positions described in the step diagrams, you should automatically develop a graceful, unhampered body motion. Swing music is aptly named, for its rhythm does seem to swing; it should make you swing along in tempo as you dance.

Many people of middle age and over think that the Lindy is strictly a teenager's dance. But the Lindy needn't be any more exerting than you care to make it.

LINDY SWING COMBINATIONS

Pattern	Number of Steps	Rhythm
(A)		
Basic Swing	4	All Steps: Slow, Slow, Quick, Quick
Release Break	4	
Bridge Break	8	
Basic Swing	4	
(B)		
Basic Turn	6	Slow, Quick, Quick
Basic Breakaway	6	Slow, Quick, Quick
Basic Swing	4	Slow, Slow, Quick, Quick
(C)		
Basic Swing	4	Slow, Slow, Quick, Quick
Bridge Break	8	Slow, Slow, Quick, Quick
Basic Breakaway	6	Slow, Quick, Quick
Basic Swing	4	Slow, Slow, Quick, Quick

CHAPTER NINETEEN

The Rumba

INTRODUCTION

THE Rumba originated with the African slaves in Cuba more than four hundred years ago. In its most primitive form it was an expressive pantomime danced by the natives under the hypnotic spell of elemental music. Even today, in the back country of Cuba, this same ritual pantomime is performed. Our ballroom Rumba, of course, is a far cry from these fascinating native demonstrations.

The Rumba was first introduced into the United States in the early 1930s. Danced properly, it is characterized by a smooth, supple hip motion and a rather heavy walking step. This gay, exotic dance contains the seeds of several cultures—African, Indian, and Spanish. Above all, the Rumba bespeaks the joy of being alive.

As you work with the Rumba step patterns, keep your knees flexed and your feet on the floor most of the time. Your steps should be small. Most of your body motion should be concentrated in your hips, as explained at the end of this chapter under "Astaire Styling." Until you have mastered all the patterns, however, you should not concern yourself with this hip motion.

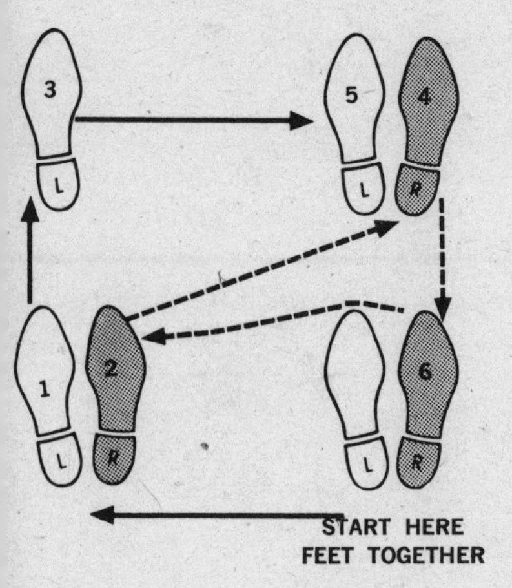

BASIC BOX STEP

Rhythm: Quick, Quick, Slow
Quick, Quick, Slow

MAN'S PART:

1. Left foot to side, Quick
2. Close with right foot, Quick
3. Left foot forward, Slow
4. Right foot forward and to side, Quick
5. Close with left foot, Quick
6. Right foot backward, Slow

NOTE: To continue pattern, bring left foot back and to side (Quick), close with right foot (Quick), left foot forward (Slow), and so forth. Take each step with the foot flat.

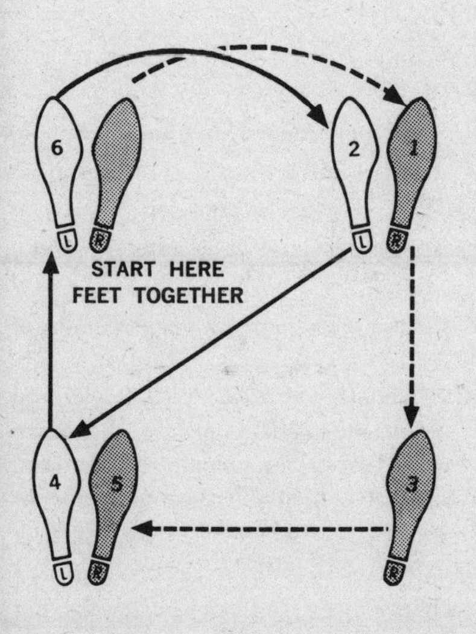

BASIC BOX STEP

Rhythm: Quick, Quick, Slow
Quick, Quick, Slow

GIRL'S PART:

1. Right foot to side, Quick
2. Close with left foot, Quick
3. Right foot backward, Slow
4. Left foot backward and to side, Quick
5. Close with right foot, Quick
6. Left foot forward, Slow

NOTE: To continue pattern, bring right foot forward and to side (Quick), close with left foot (Quick), right foot backward (Slow), and so forth.

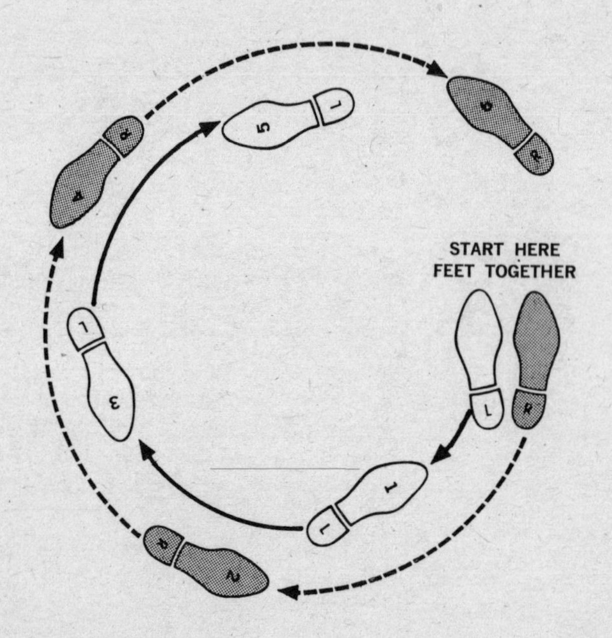

OPEN CUBAN WALK

Rhythm: Quick, Quick, Slow
Quick, Quick, Slow

MAN'S PART:

1. Left foot backward, Quick (turn toe slightly inward to begin turn to right)
2. Right foot backward, Quick (turn toe slightly outward to continue turn to right)
3. Left foot backward, Slow (turn toe inward, continue turn to right)
4. Right foot backward, Quick (continue turn to right)
5. Left foot backward, Quick (continue turn to right)
6. Right foot backward, Slow (complete turn to right)

NOTE: This step is executed turning to the right, or in a straight backward direction. Practice it moving straight until the pattern is mastered. Then, gradually turn to the right, taking care not to make the steps too large. Before starting the Open Cuban Walk, the man dances one complete Basic Box Step, then releases his right hand hold, so that the Cuban Walk is danced in the open position.

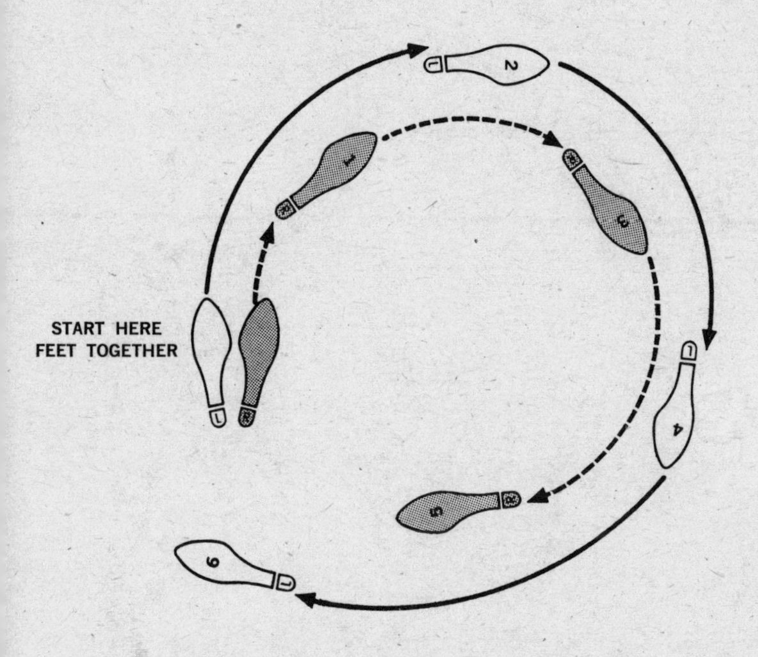

OPEN CUBAN WALK

Rhythm: Quick, Quick, Slow
Quick, Quick, Slow

GIRL'S PART

1. Right foot forward, Quick (turn toe slightly outward to begin turn to right)
2. Left foot forward, Quick (turn toe inward to continue turn to right)
3. Right foot forward, Slow (turn toe outward, continue turn to right)
4. Left foot forward, Quick (continue turn to right)
5. Right foot forward, Quick (continue turn to right)
6. Left foot forward, Slow (complete turn to right)

NOTE: See note under man's part.

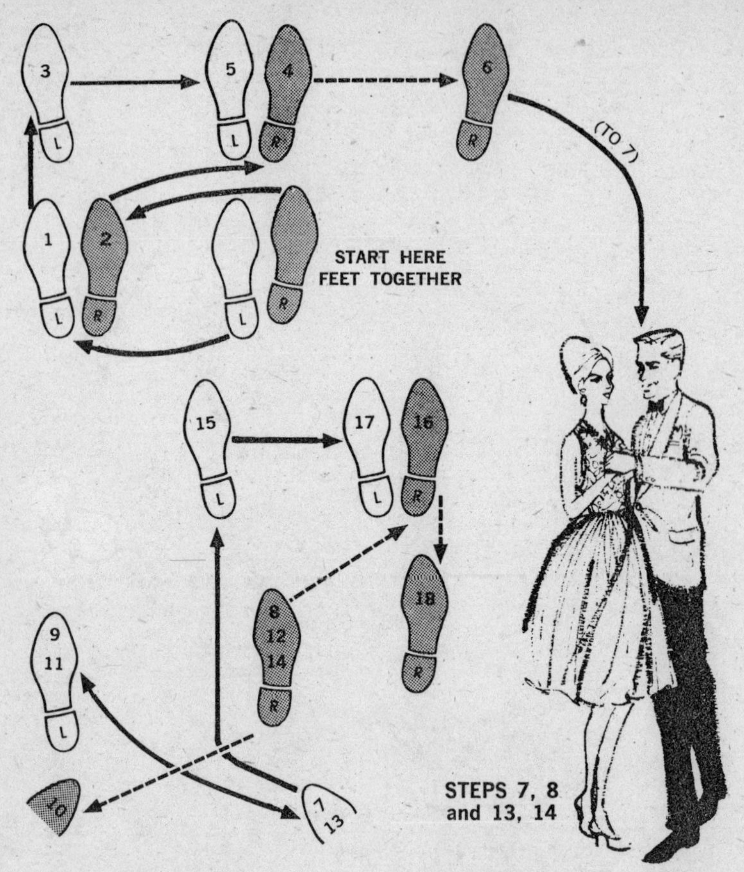

SIDE BREAK

Rhythm: Quick, Quick, Slow
Quick, Quick, Slow

MAN'S PART:

1. Left foot to side, Quick
2. Close with right foot, Quick
3. Left foot forward, Slow
4. Right foot forward and to side, Quick
5. Close with left foot, Quick
6. Right foot to side, Slow
7. Left foot backward, Quick (place left foot behind right heel, putting weight on ball of left foot)
8. Right foot in place, Quick
9. Left foot forward and to side, Slow
10. Right foot backward, Quick (place right foot behind left heel, putting weight on ball of left foot)
11. Left foot in place, Quick
12. Right foot forward and to side, Slow
13. Left foot backward, Quick (place left foot behind right heel, putting weight on ball of left foot)
14. Right foot in place, Quick
15. Left foot forward, Slow
16. Right foot forward and to side, Quick
17. Close with left foot, Quick
18. Right foot backward, Slow

NOTE: Steps 7 and 8 are danced in left open position. Steps 10 and 11 are danced in right open position. Use the 9th step to make the change of positions. Steps 13 and 14 are danced in left open position. Steps 15, 16, 17, and 18 are danced in closed position. (See drawings.)

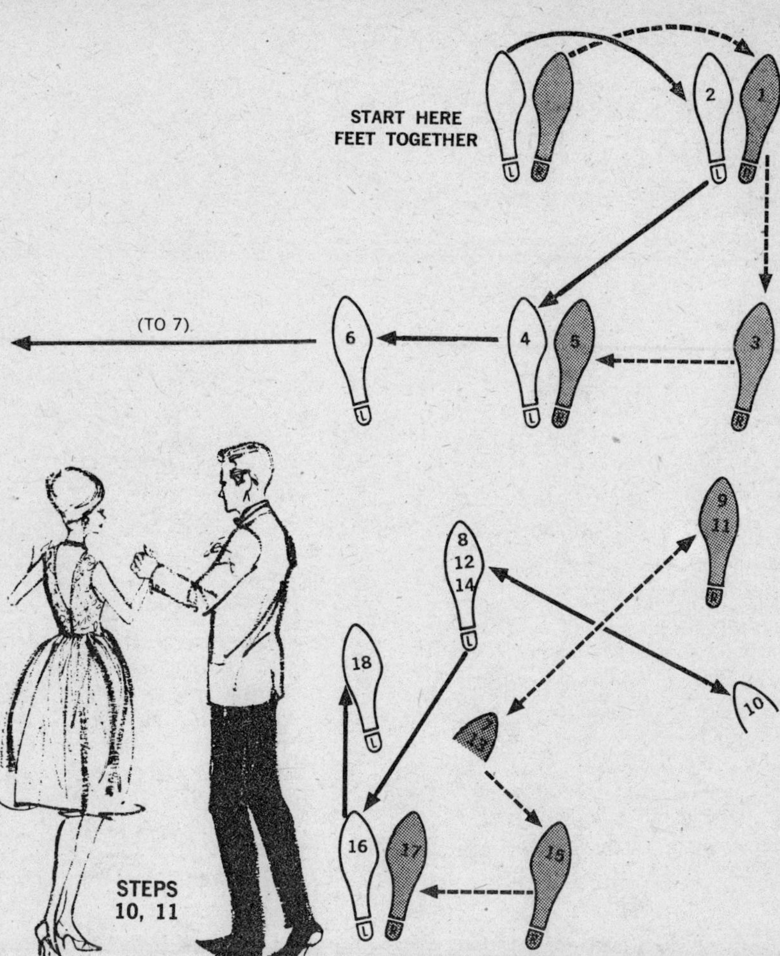

SIDE BREAK

Rhythm: Quick, Quick, Slow
Quick, Quick, Slow

GIRL'S PART:

1. Right foot to side, Quick
2. Close with left foot, Quick
3. Right foot backward, Slow
4. Left foot backward and to side, Quick
5. Close with right foot, Quick
6. Left foot to side, Slow
7. Right foot backward, Quick (place right foot behind left heel, putting weight on ball of right foot)
8. Left foot in place, Quick
9. Right foot forward and to side, Slow
10. Left foot backward, Quick (place left foot behind right heel, putting weight on ball of left foot)
11. Right foot in place, Quick
12. Left foot forward and to side, Slow
13. Right foot backward, Quick (place right foot behind left heel, putting weight on ball of right foot)
14. Left foot in place, Quick
15. Right foot backward, Slow
16. Left foot backward and to side, Quick
17. Close with right foot, Quick
18. Left foot forward, Slow

NOTE: See note under man's part.

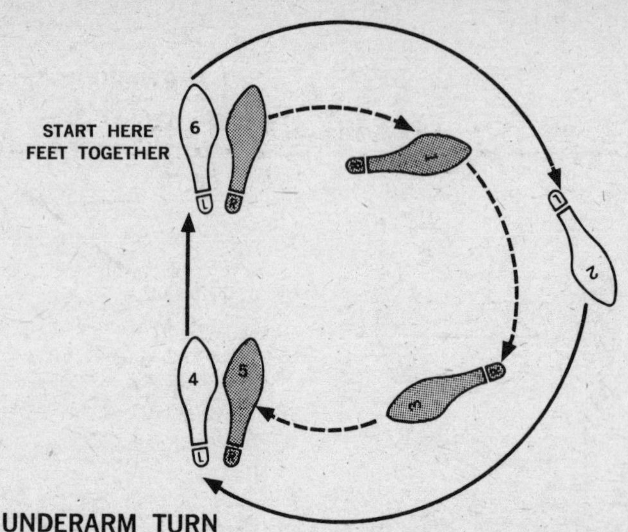

UNDERARM TURN

Rhythm: Quick, Quick, Slow
Quick, Quick, Slow

GIRL'S PART:

1. Right foot to side, Quick (point toe outward to start turn)
2. Left foot forward, Quick (continue turn as illustrated in diagram)
3. Right foot forward, Slow (continue turn as illustrated)
4. Left foot around to side, Quick (continue turn as illustrated)
5. Close with right foot, Quick (complete turn by bringing feet together)
6. Left foot forward, Slow

NOTE: Only the girl executes the Underarm Turn. The man dances two complete Basic Box Steps, leading his partner underarm on the first step of the second Basic Box Step pattern. The girl dances one complete Basic Box Step before taking first underarm step. (See drawings.)

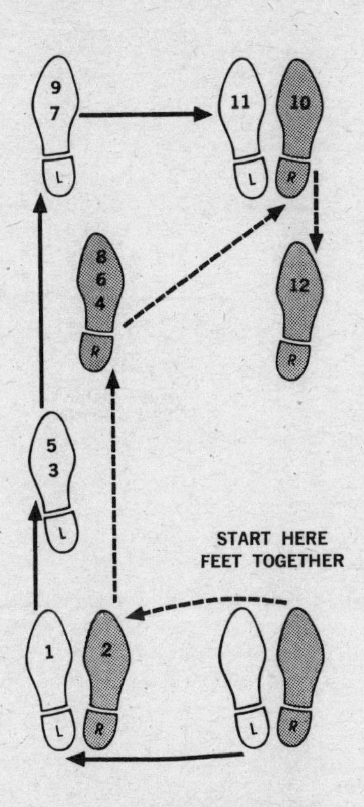

FORWARD ROCK

Rhythm: Quick, Quick, Slow
Quick, Quick, Slow

MAN'S PART:

1. Left foot to side, Quick
2. Close with right foot, Quick
3. Left foot forward, Slow
4. Right foot forward, Quick
5. Left foot in place, Quick
6. Right foot in place, Slow
7. Left foot forward, Quick
8. Right foot in place, Quick
9. Left foot in place, Slow
10. Right foot forward and to side, Quick
11. Close with left foot, Quick
12. Right foot backward, Slow

NOTE: As the man does the Forward Rock, the girl does the Backward Rock. Each partner should learn the pattern moving forward and backward. Take small steps throughout. Caution must be taken not to rock the upper part of the body; keep it motionless, and rock only with the feet.

BACKWARD ROCK

Rhythm: Quick, Quick, Slow
Quick, Quick, Slow

GIRL'S PART:

1. Right foot to side, Quick
2. Close with left foot, Quick
3. Right foot backward, Slow
4. Left foot backward, Quick
5. Right foot in place, Quick
6. Left foot in place, Slow
7. Right foot backward, Quick
8. Left foot in place, Quick
9. Right foot in place, Slow
10. Left foot backward and to side, Quick
11. Close with right foot, Quick
12. Left foot forward, Slow

NOTE: See note under man's part.

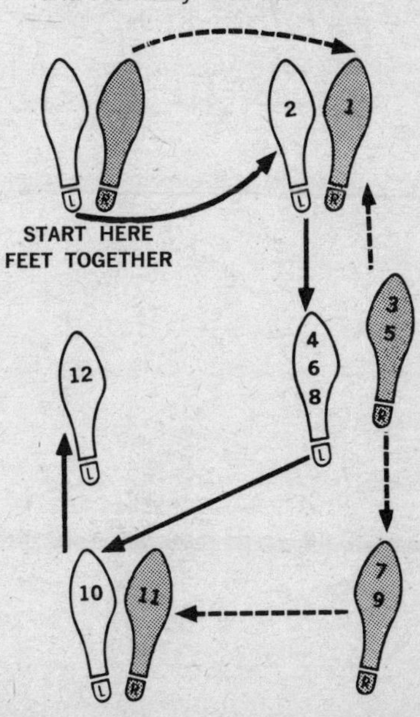

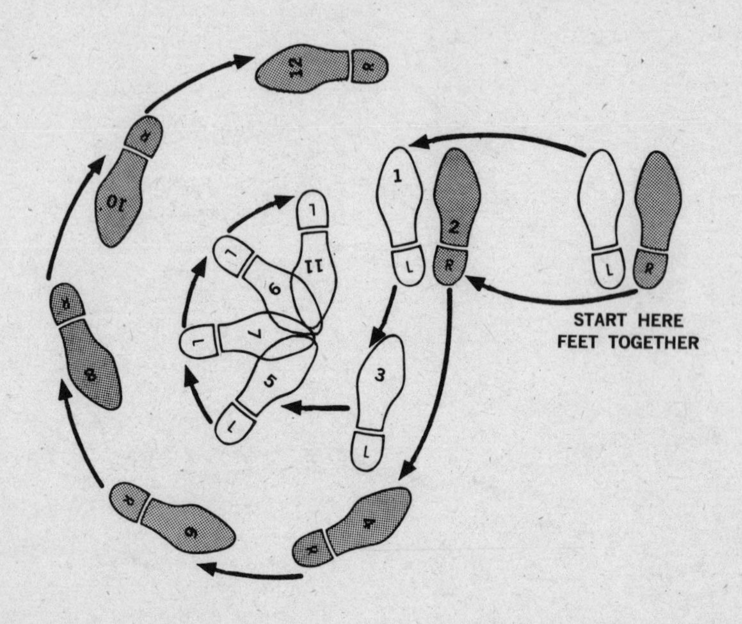

BACKWARD RIGHT TURN

Rhythm: Quick, Quick, Slow
Quick, Quick, Slow

MAN'S PART

1. Left foot to side, Quick
2. Close with right foot, Quick
3. Left foot backward, Slow (turn toe slightly inward to begin turn to right)
4. Right foot backward, Quick (turn toe slightly outward to continue turn to right)
5. Left foot to side, Quick (turning to right)
6. Right foot backward, Slow
7. Left foot to side (small step), Quick
8. Right foot backward, Quick (from here to end of pattern, simply pass the right foot backward around pivoting left foot)
9. Left foot to side (small step), Slow
10. Right foot backward, Quick
11. Left foot to side (small step), Quick
12. Right foot backward, Slow (turn is completed)

NOTE: As the man executes the Backward Right Turn, the girl does a Forward Right Turn. After the 12th step is taken, the man steps to the side with his left foot and dances the Basic Box Step.

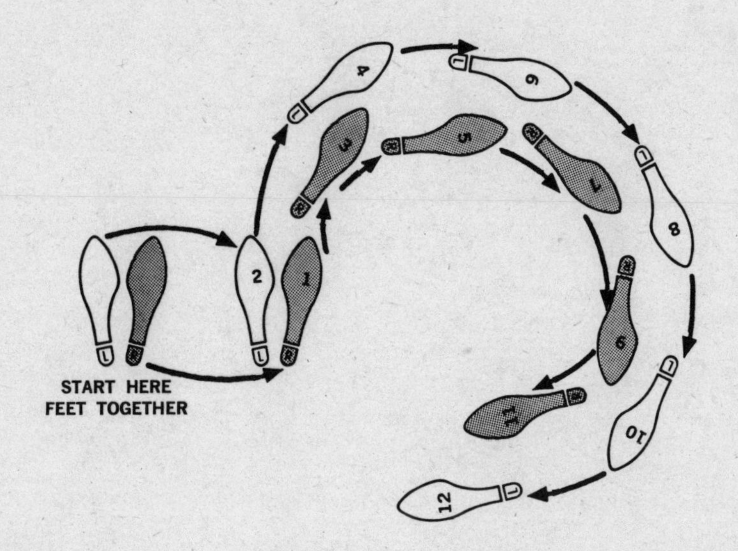

FORWARD RIGHT TURN

Rhythm: Quick, Quick, Slow
Quick, Quick, Slow

GIRL'S PART

1. Right foot to side, Quick
2. Close with left foot, Quick
3. Right foot forward, Slow (start turn to right by pointing toe out)
4. Left foot forward, Quick (continue turn by pointing left toe inward)
5. Right foot forward, Quick (continue turn)
6. Left foot forward, Slow (continue turn)
7. Right foot forward, Quick (continue turn)
8. Left foot forward, Quick (continue turn)
9. Right foot forward, Slow (continue turn)
10. Left foot forward, Quick (continue turn)
11. Right foot forward, Quick (continue turn)
12. Left foot forward, Slow (turn is completed)

NOTE: In effect, the girl simply walks forward to make her turn. When dancing with a partner, however, it becomes necessary for the girl to make her turn more compact, dancing her forward steps in a small circle. Cutting down on the size of her steps will make it easier for the man to lead her.

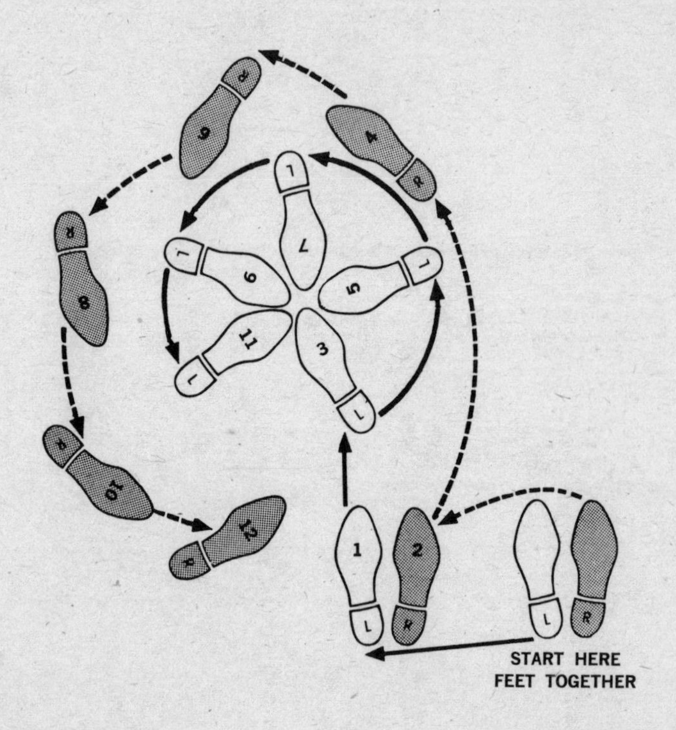

FORWARD LEFT TURN

Rhythm: Quick, Quick, Slow
Quick, Quick, Slow

MAN'S PART

1. Left foot to side, Quick
2. Close with right foot, Quick
3. Left foot forward, Slow (point toe slightly outward to begin turn to left)
4. Right foot forward, Quick (point toe slightly inward to continue turn to left)
5. Left foot forward (small step), Quick (from here to end of pattern, keep left toe pointed to center of turning figure; see diagram)
6. Right foot forward, Slow (from here to end of pattern, simply pass right foot forward around pivoting left foot)
7. Left foot forward (small step), Quick
8. Right foot forward, Quick
9. Left foot forward (small step), Slow
10. Right foot forward, Quick
11. Left foot forward (small step), Quick
12. Right foot forward, Slow (turn is completed)

NOTE: As the man executes the Forward Left Turn, the girl does a Backward Left Turn. After the 12th step is taken, the man steps to the side with his left foot and dances the Basic Box Step.

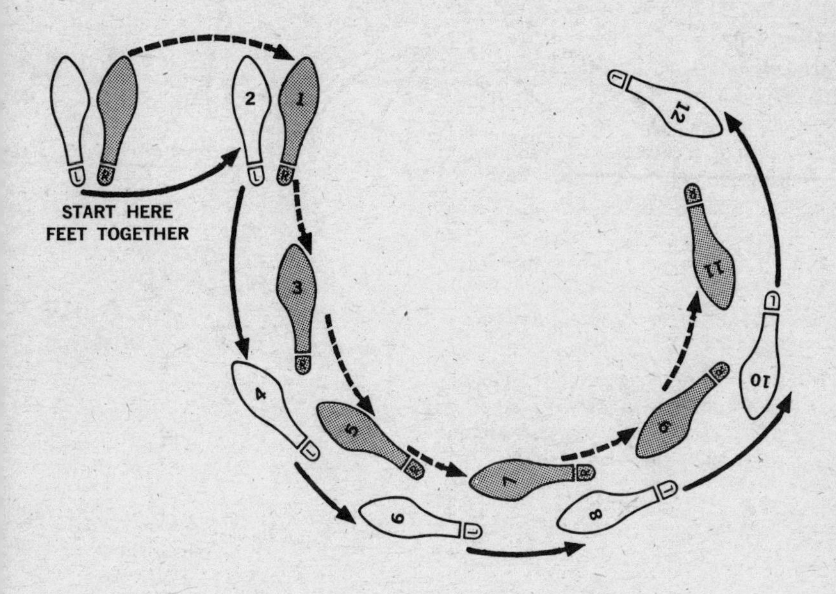

BACKWARD LEFT TURN

Rhythm: Quick, Quick, Slow
Quick, Quick, Slow

GIRLS PART

1. Right foot to side, Quick
2. Close with left foot, Quick
3. Right foot backward, Slow (point toe slightly inward to begin turn to left)
4. Left foot backward, Quick (continue to left)
5. Right foot backward, Quick (continue turn to left)
6. Left foot backward, Slow (continue turn)
7. Right foot backward, Quick (continue turn)
8. Left foot backward, Quick (continue turn)
9. Right foot backward, Slow (continue turn)
10. Left foot backward, Quick (continue turn)
11. Right foot backward, Quick (continue turn)
12. Left foot backward, Slow (turn is completed)

NOTE: In effect, the girl simply walks backward to make her turn. When dancing with a partner, however, it becomes necessary for the girl to make her turn more compact, dancing her backward steps in a small circle. Cutting down on the size of her steps will make it easier for the man to lead her.

CUBAN LEFT TURN

Rhythm: Quick, Quick, Slow
Quick, Quick, Slow

MAN'S PART

1. Left foot to side, Quick
2. Right foot backward, Quick (begin turning to left)
3. Left foot in place, Slow (turn toe out to the left)
4. Right foot forward and to side, Quick (point toe inward)
5. Left foot forward, Quick (point toe outward)
6. Right foot in place, Slow (turn is completed)

NOTE: Turn gradually to the left, making a quarter turn between steps 1 and 6. This step may be repeated as many times as desired.

START HERE
FEET TOGETHER

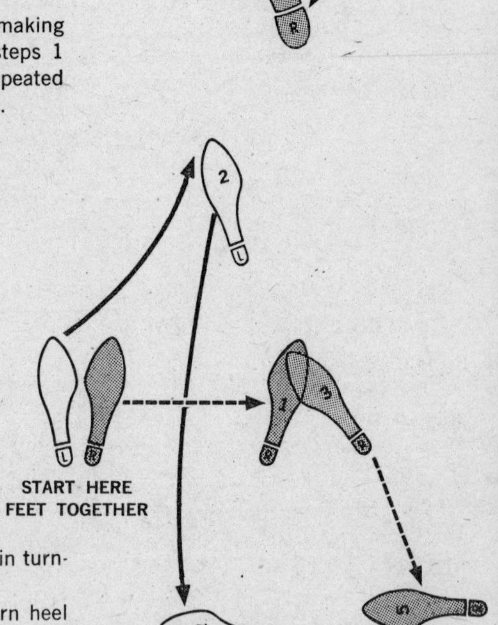

CUBAN LEFT TURN

Rhythm: Quick, Quick, Slow
Quick, Quick, Slow

GIRL'S PART

1. Right foot to side, Quick
2. Left foot forward, Quick (begin turning to left)
3. Right foot in place, Slow (turn heel out)
4. Left foot backward and to side, Quick (point toe outward)
5. Right foot backward, Quick (point toe inward)
6. Left foot in place, Slow (turn is completed)

NOTE: See note under man's part.

Astaire Styling: The Cuban Motion

As with all dances of Cuban origin, such as the Mambo and Cha Cha Cha, you should concentrate your body motion in your hips. Keep them continually moving horizontally, while the top part of your body remains almost motionless, though relaxed and limber.

One way to achieve this motion is to imagine that your body is a pendulum. Your torso is the stem of the pendulum and your hip region is the part that swings to and fro. The worst mistake you can make is to overdo this motion. Try to move your hips smoothly and subtly from side to side.

Review the description of Cuban motion given at the end of the Cha Cha Cha lesson (Chapter 16). Remember, as long as you bend the proper knee with each step taken, your hips should move themselves automatically. Practice all the principles of follow-through and take smaller steps than usual. The successful Rumba dancer always has perfect control of his body motion. Therefore, you should practice all step patterns for the Rumba slowly and individually until you have mastered the art of moving your hips in the graceful Cuban tradition.

RUMBA COMBINATIONS

Pattern	Number of Steps	Rhythm
(A)		
Basic Box Step	6	
Side Break	18	All steps: Quick, Quick, Slow
Underarm Turn	12	
(B)		
Forward Rock (Girl does Backward Rock)	12	
Backward Right Turn	12	All steps: Quick, Quick, Slow
Basic Box Step	6	
(C)		
Cuban Left Turn	12	
Forward Left Turn	12	
Basic Box Step	6	All steps: Quick, Quick, Slow
Open Cuban Walk	6	
Basic Box Step	6	

CHAPTER TWENTY

The Tango

INTRODUCTION

IN the midst of the greatest period of dance evolution in American history—1910 to 1914—the Tango made its first appearance. It instantly struck the fancy of a dance-conscious public, for its intriguing, asymmetrical, and sophisticated patterns added romance and suavity to the nation's dancing scene.

The Tango has no clearly defined origin; it may have originated in Argentina, Brazil, Spain, or Mexico. Descended from an early Spanish folk dance, the Milogna, and bearing traces of Moorish and Arabic ancestry, the Tango first came to be known, as such, early in the twentieth century in Argentina. It was being danced, however, under various other names throughout all of Latin America.

For the past twenty-five years or so, the four-beat Tango rhythm has endured and has continued to enjoy undiminished favor everywhere. It is a dramatic dance with measured crossing and flexing steps and poised pauses. Perhaps one reason for its widespread popularity is that it is danced close to the partner.

The Tango is one of the most highly stylized ballroom dances. Follow-through and contrabody motion are both indispensable. Footwork must be meticulously executed, with the knees flexed and the dancer's weight centered over the instep.

When dancing the Tango, the foot should be placed flat on the floor when progressing forward. Stand straight and hold your hips close to your partner. Use straight follow-through when moving forward or backward; use angular follow-through when moving sideward.

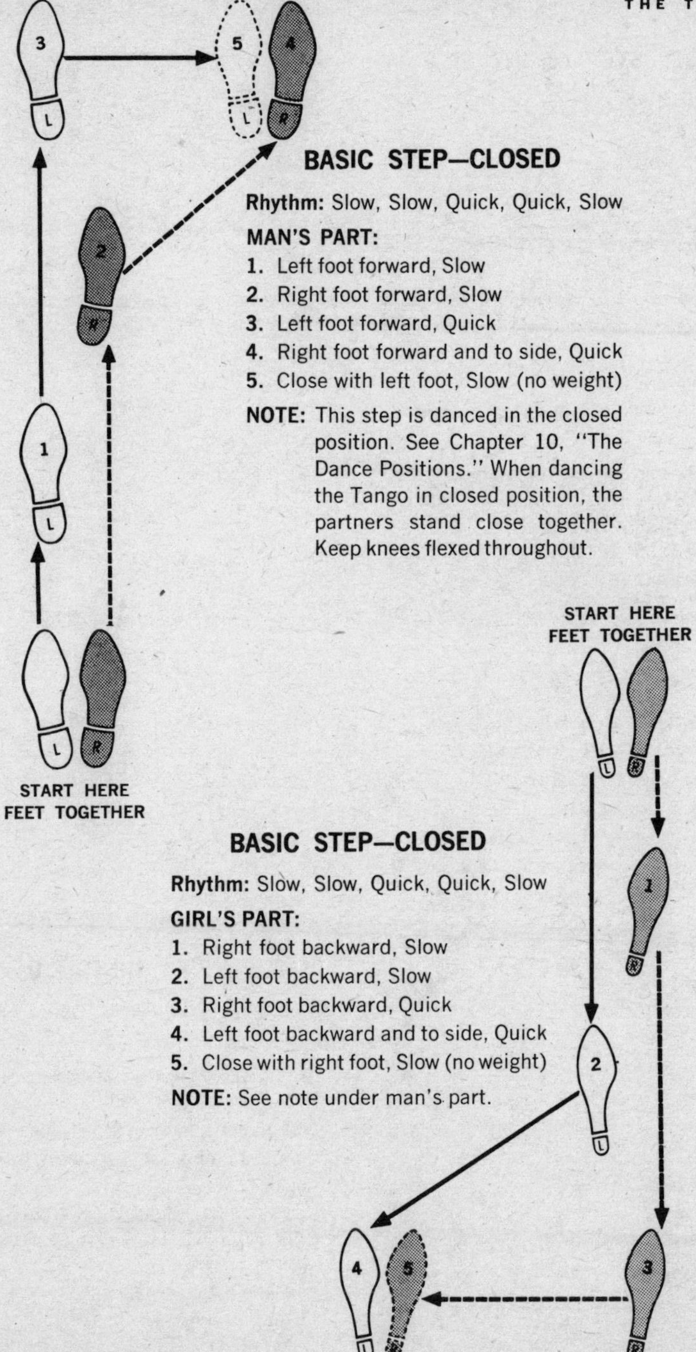

BASIC STEP—CLOSED

Rhythm: Slow, Slow, Quick, Quick, Slow

MAN'S PART:

1. Left foot forward, Slow
2. Right foot forward, Slow
3. Left foot forward, Quick
4. Right foot forward and to side, Quick
5. Close with left foot, Slow (no weight)

NOTE: This step is danced in the closed position. See Chapter 10, "The Dance Positions." When dancing the Tango in closed position, the partners stand close together. Keep knees flexed throughout.

BASIC STEP—CLOSED

Rhythm: Slow, Slow, Quick, Quick, Slow

GIRL'S PART:

1. Right foot backward, Slow
2. Left foot backward, Slow
3. Right foot backward, Quick
4. Left foot backward and to side, Quick
5. Close with right foot, Slow (no weight)

NOTE: See note under man's part.

BASIC STEP—RIGHT SIDE

Rhythm: Slow, Slow, Quick, Quick, Slow

MAN'S PART:

1. Left foot forward diagonal, Slow (in right side position)
2. Right foot forward, Slow (Place heel directly in front of left toe in right side position)
3. Left foot forward, Quick (place heel directly in front of right toe in closed position)
4. Right foot forward and to side, Quick
5. Close with left foot, Slow (no weight)

NOTE: This pattern is a slight variation of the Basic Step. The first two steps are danced in right side position, rather than in closed position. See Chapter 10, "The Dance Positions."

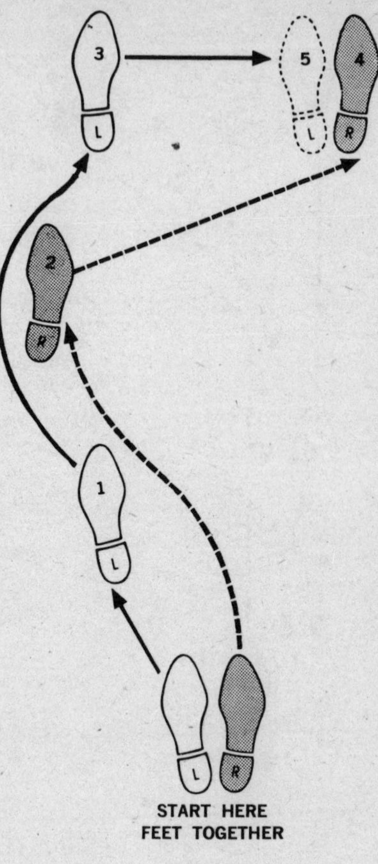

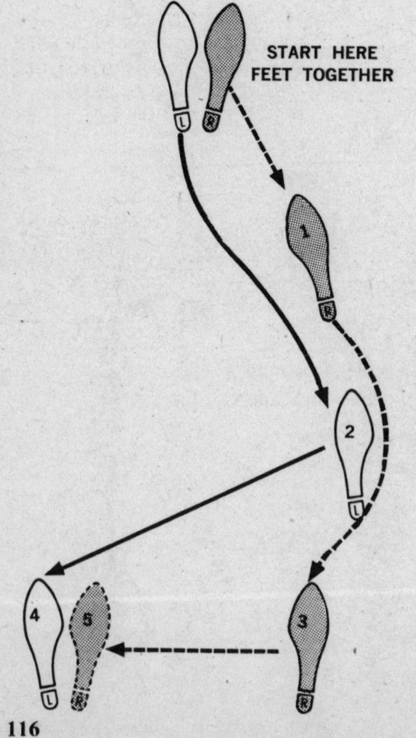

BASIC STEP—RIGHT SIDE

Rhythm: Slow, Slow, Quick, Quick, Slow

GIRL'S PART:

1. Right foot backward diagonal, Slow (in right side position)
2. Left foot backward, Slow (place toe directly behind right heel in right side position)
3. Right foot backward, Quick (place toe directly behind left heel in closed position)
4. Left foot backward and to side, Quick
5. Close with right foot, Slow (no weight)

NOTE: See note under man's part.

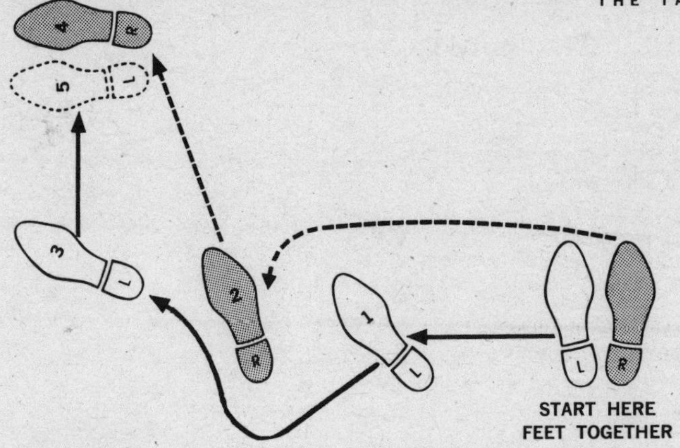

PROMENADE

Rhythm: Slow, Slow, Quick, Quick, Slow

MAN'S PART:

1. Left foot to side, Slow (in left open position)
2. Right foot forward, Slow (cross in front of left foot in left open position)
3. Left foot forward, Quick (in closed position; see diagram)
4. Right foot forward and to side, Quick
5. Close with left foot, Slow (no weight)

NOTE: This pattern is a slight variation of the Basic Step. The first two steps are danced in left open position rather than in closed position. See Chapter 10, "The Dance Positions." (See drawings.)

STEP 1 STEP 2 STEP 3

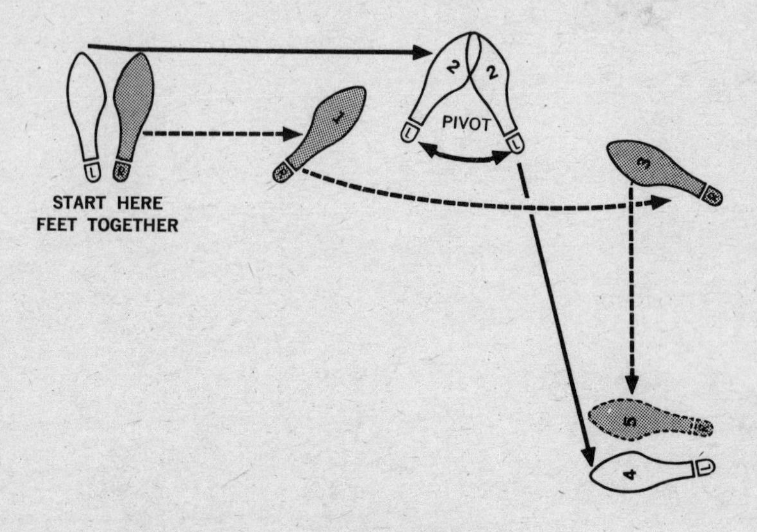

PROMENADE

Rhythm: Slow, Slow, Quick, Quick, Slow

GIRL'S PART:

1. Right foot to side, Slow (point toe out in left open position)
2. Left foot forward and pivot to left, Slow (cross in front of right foot in left open position)
3. Right foot backward, Quick (cross behind left foot; as you move right foot backward, pivot on the toe of your left foot—see diagram—in closed position)
4. Left foot backward and to side, Quick
5. Close with right foot, Slow (no weight)

NOTE: See note under man's part. (On the second foot movement, the girl makes a slight pivot to the left, so that she can take her third step in closed position.) (See drawings.)

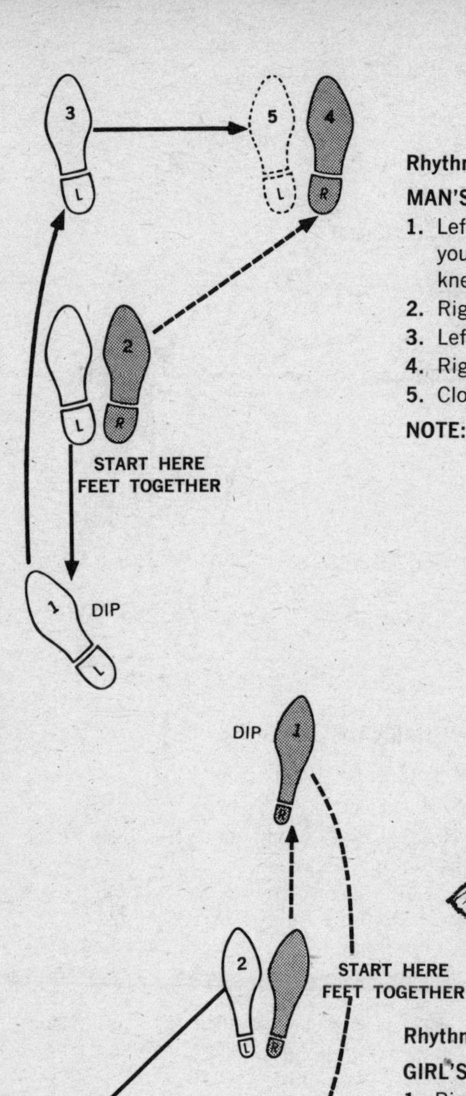

CORTÉ

Rhythm: Slow, Slow, Quick, Quick, Slow

MAN'S PART:

1. Left foot backward, Slow (as you put your weight down on foot, bend your knee and gracefully dip)
2. Right foot in place, Slow
3. Left foot forward, Quick
4. Right foot forward and to side, Quick
5. Close with left foot, Slow (no weight)

NOTE: As the Corté (or Dip) is taken, the man turns his left foot out slightly so that his left knee will not be in a direct line with his partner's right knee. (See drawing.)

CORTÉ

Rhythm: Slow, Slow, Quick, Quick, Slow

GIRL'S PART:

1. Right foot forward, Slow (As you put your weight down on foot, bend your knee and gracefully dip)
2. Left foot in place, Slow
3. Right foot backward, Quick
4. Left foot backward and to side, Quick
5. Close with right foot, Slow (no weight)

NOTE: As the Corté (or Dip) is taken, stretch the left toe backward so that the left leg is straight and the left heel is raised from the ground. (See drawing.)

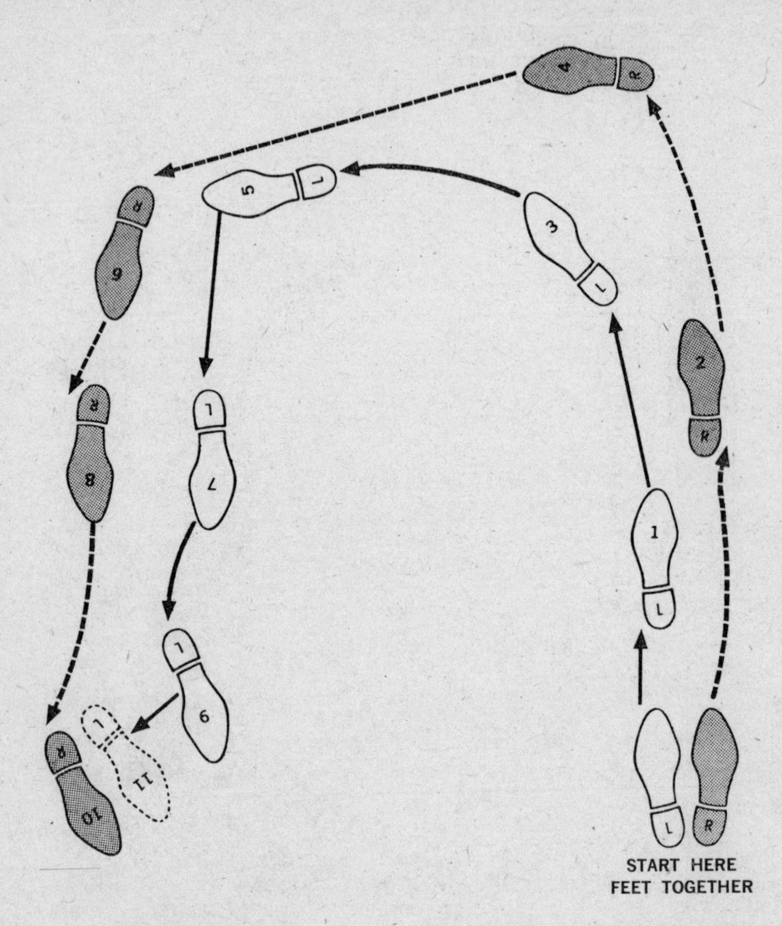

RUNNING STEP

Rhythm: Slow, Slow, Quick, Quick
Slow, Slow, Quick, Quick
Quick, Quick, Slow

MAN'S PART:

1. Left foot forward, Slow
2. Right foot forward, Slow
3. Left foot forward, Quick (point toe slightly to begin turn to left)
4. Right foot forward and to side, Quick (point toe to left)
5. Left foot forward, Slow (point toe to left)
6. Right foot forward, Slow (pass foot around left foot, turning toe to left)
7. Left foot forward, Quick
8. Right foot forward and to side, Quick (feet are apart and parallel)
9. Left foot forward, Quick (point toe slightly to left)
10. Right foot forward and to side, Quick (point toe slightly to left, so feet are parallel)
11. Close with left foot, Slow (no weight)

NOTE: The running steps may be danced either in a straight line or turning gradually to the left.

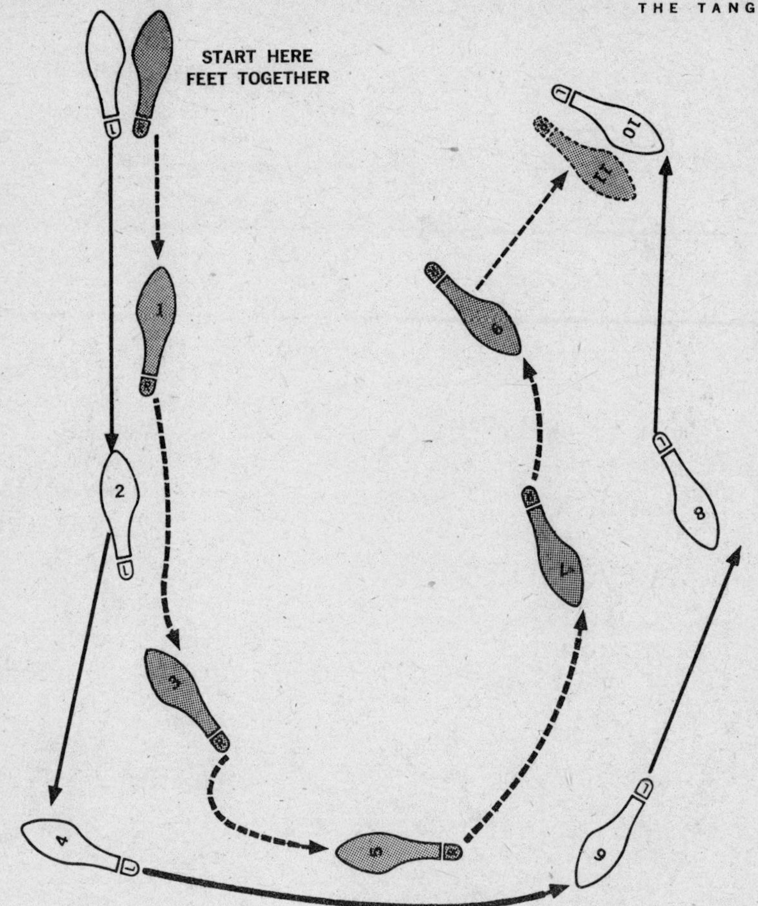

RUNNING STEP

Rhythm: Slow, Slow, Quick, Quick
Slow, Slow, Quick, Quick
Quick, Quick, Slow

GIRL'S PART:

1. Right foot backward, Slow
2. Left foot backward, Slow
3. Right foot backward, Quick (begin turn to left)
4. Left foot backward and to side, Quick (point toe to left)
5. Right foot backward, Slow (pass foot along curved line, as in diagram, pointing toe to left)
6. Left foot backward, Slow (pass foot around right foot, turning toe to left)
7. Right foot backward, Quick (turn toe to left)
8. Left foot backward and to side, Quick (feet are apart and parallel)
9. Right foot backward, Quick (point toe slightly to left)
10. Left foot backward and to side, Quick (point toe slightly to left, so feet are parallel)
11. Close with left foot, Slow (no weight)

NOTE: See note under man's part.

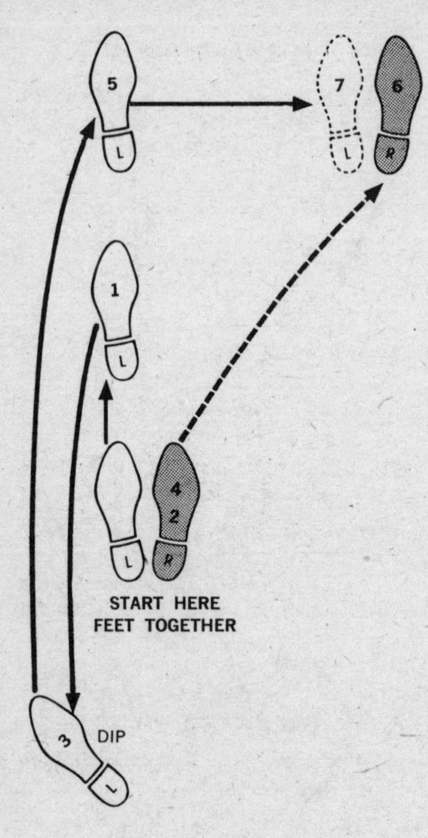

ROCK AND CORTÉ

Rhythm: Quick, Quick, Slow, Slow
Quick, Quick, Slow

MAN'S PART:

1. Left foot forward, Quick
2. Right foot in place, Quick
3. Left foot backward, Slow (execute dip as described in Corté)
4. Right foot in place, Slow
5. Left foot forward, Quick
6. Right foot forward and to side, Quick
7. Close with left foot, Slow (no weight)

NOTE: When dancing the Rock and Corté, use contrabody movement on step 1. Apply the principles of a graceful Corte, as described in the Corté Step.

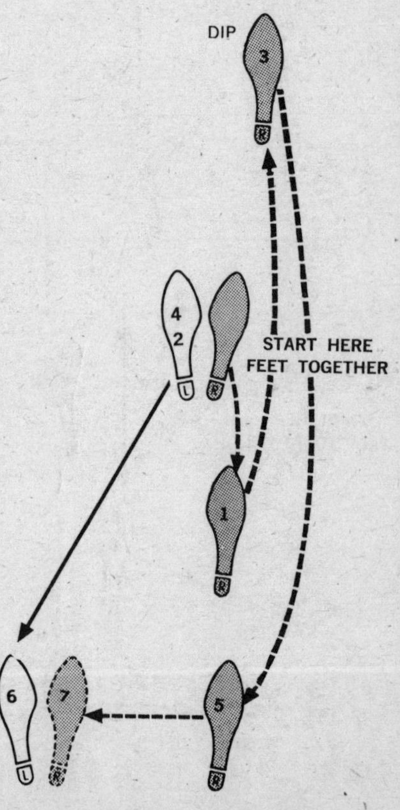

ROCK AND CORTÉ

Rhythm: Quick, Quick, Slow, Slow
Quick, Quick, Slow

GIRL'S PART:

1. Right foot backward, Quick
2. Left foot in place, Quick
3. Right foot forward, Slow (execute dip as described in Corté)
4. Left foot in place, Slow
5. Right foot backward, Quick
6. Left foot backward and to side, Quick
7. Close with right foot, Slow (no weight)

NOTE: See note under man's part.

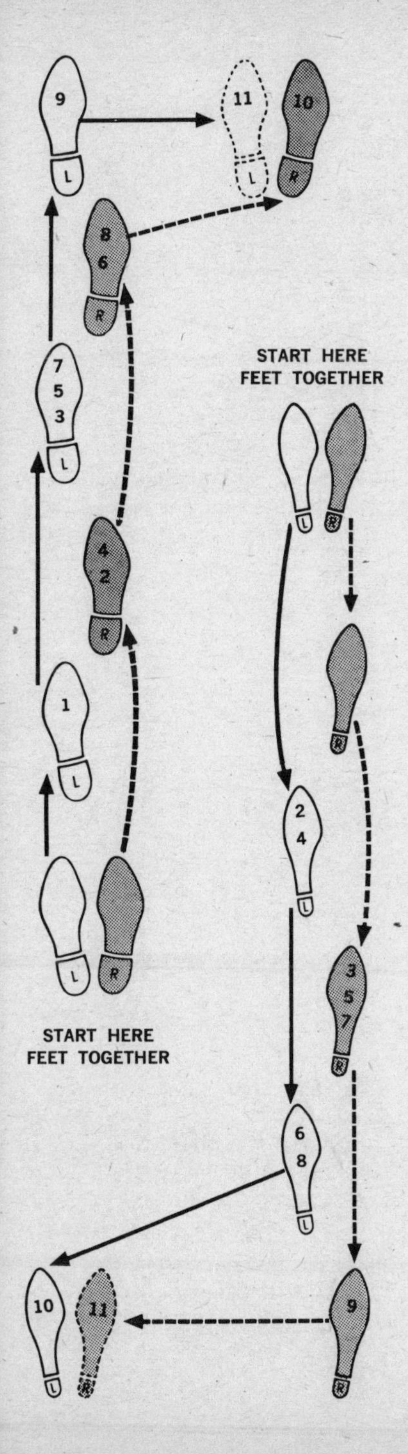

FORWARD ROCK

Rhythm: Slow, Slow, Quick, Quick, Slow
Quick, Quick, Slow
Quick, Quick, Slow

MAN'S PART:

1. Left foot forward, Slow
2. Right foot forward, Slow
3. Left foot forward, Quick
4. Right foot in place, Quick
5. Left foot in place, Slow
6. Right foot forward, Quick
7. Left foot in place, Quick
8. Right foot in place, Slow
9. Left foot forward, Quick
10. Right foot forward and to side, Quick
11. Close with left foot, Slow (no weight)

NOTE: When dancing the Forward Rock, use contrabody movement on Steps 3 and 6. The actual rocking steps (steps 3 through 8) are small steps. Both knees are flexed.

BACKWARD ROCK

Rhythm: Slow, Slow, Quick, Quick, Slow
Quick, Quick, Slow
Quick, Quick, Slow

GIRL'S PART:

1. Right foot backward, Slow
2. Left foot backward, Slow
3. Right foot backward, Quick
4. Left foot in place, Quick
5. Right foot in place, Slow
6. Left foot backward, Quick
7. Right foot in place, Quick
8. Left foot in place, Slow
9. Right foot backward, Quick
10. Left foot backward and to side, Quick
11. Close with right foot, Slow (no weight)

NOTE: See note under man's part. For the girl, it applies, of course, to Backward Rock.

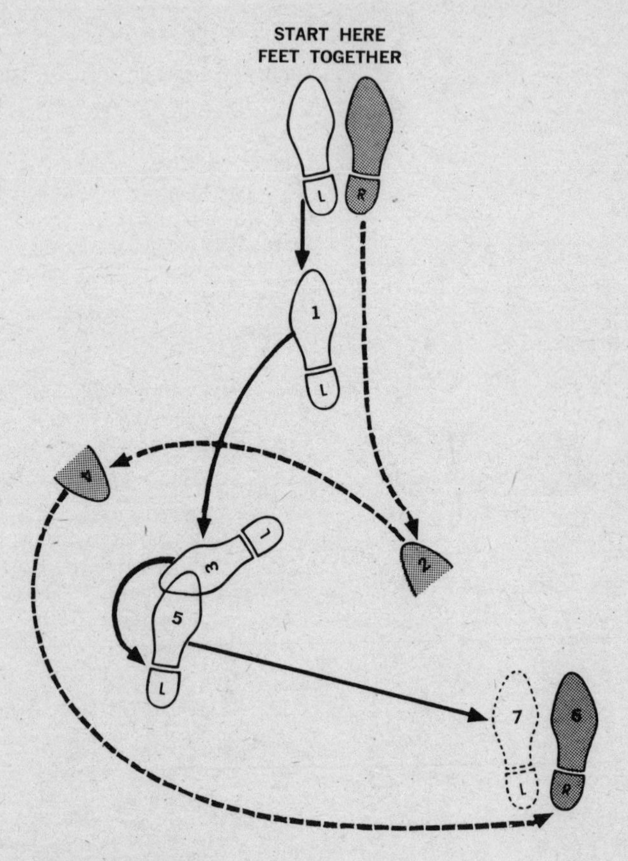

AD-LIB TURN

Rhythm: Slow, Quick, Quick, Quick
Quick, Quick, Quick

MAN'S PART:

1. Left foot backward, Slow
2. Right foot backward, Quick (put weight on ball of foot and begin turning to left)
3. Left foot forward, Quick (turn toe to left, as in diagram)
4. Right foot backward, Quick (bring foot around and behind left foot, pointing toe inward; put weight on ball of right foot)
5. Left foot forward, Quick (end turn to left)
6. Right foot forward and to side, Quick (bring foot around and behind left foot, pointing toe inward)
7. Close with left foot, Quick (no weight)

NOTE: Begin turning to the left on step 2, and continue turn until the end of step 5. One complete left turn is made between steps 2 and 5.

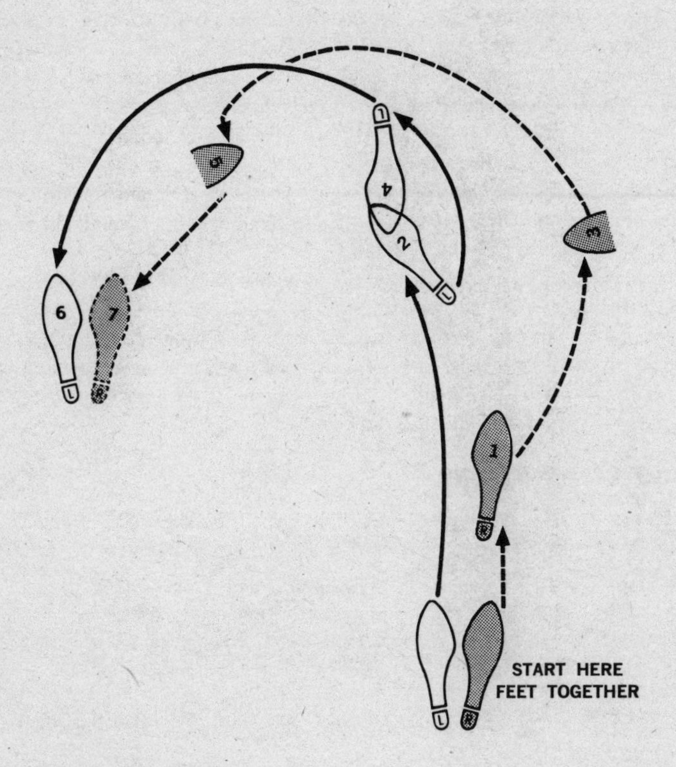

AD-LIB TURN

Rhythm: Slow, Quick, Quick, Quick
Quick, Quick, Quick

GIRL'S PART:

1. Right foot forward, Slow
2. Left foot forward, Quick (point toe slightly to left)
3. Right foot backward, Quick (turn toe to left putting weight on ball of right foot)
4. Left foot forward, Quick (turning to left)
5. Right foot backward, Quick (swing foot around and behind left foot, pointing toe inward; put weight on ball of right foot)
6. Left foot backward and to side, Quick (swing foot around and to side of right foot; see diagram)
7. Close with right foot, Quick (no weight)

NOTE: See note under man's part.

Astaire Styling: The Tango

The general styling of the Tango includes many controlled body movements. The more advanced the dancer, the more refinements his dancing will include. As a beginner, you should pay attention to a few simple points of Tango style and body motion. Then, as you become more proficient and your understanding of the dance matures, you can embellish your basic technique.

First, keep your body tall, with your weight placed over the insteps of your feet and your knees flexed. Body movement is that of walking, with no up and down motion. Every slow step should be held until the last possible moment before moving the opposite leg. The observance of this rule will do more than almost anything else to make your Tango look like a Tango.

Key your movements strictly to the music, timing your pauses and stops. Be sure to end a movement when the music stops.

Finally, avoid dancing too many patterns in the open position. Both the man and the girl should keep the upper parts of their bodies in close contact as much of the time as possible. Whenever you step into a turn, the lower parts of your bodies—from the waist down—should glide through evenly and in unison.

TANGO COMBINATIONS

Pattern	Number of Steps	Rhythm
(A)		
Basic Step—Closed	5	Slow, Slow, Quick, Quick, Slow
Corté	5	Slow, Slow, Quick, Quick, Slow
Forward Rock	11	Slow, Slow, Quick, Quick, Slow—Quick, Quick, Slow—Quick, Quick, Slow
(B)		
Rock and Corté	7	Quick, Quick, Slow, Slow, Quick, Quick, Slow
Basic Step—Right Side	5	Slow, Slow, Quick, Quick, Slow
Running Step	11	Slow, Slow, Quick, Quick—Slow, Slow, Quick, Quick—Quick, Quick, Slow
(C)		
Ad-Lib Turn	7	Slow, Quick, Quick, Quick, Quick, Quick, Quick
Promenade	5	Slow, Slow, Quick, Quick, Slow
Corté	5	Slow, Slow, Quick, Quick, Slow

CHAPTER TWENTY-ONE

The Samba

INTRODUCTION

WHEN the Samba was introduced into the United States in 1929, it became an overnight sensation. Like many other Brazilian dances, the music is an amalgamation of African and Latin American rhythms which have come to be adorned with expressive melodic lines. In form, the Samba is a serenade; the repetitions of its melody are interrupted continually by the strumming of a guitar or other stringed instrument. The dance first became famous in Rio de Janeiro, and later its intoxicating rhythm was taken up by serious Latin American composers.

The Samba is gay and lighthearted, as performed today in the United States. It brings to mind pictures of a gala fiesta in Rio. In its native land, however, the Samba is usually danced to a moderately slow tempo which contrasts vividly with the spirited version favored in this country. In the beginning you are advised to practice Samba steps to a slow tempo. As you perfect your technique and gain confidence, you can increase the tempo progressively.

The Samba is a dance with many contrasting movements, which add to its appeal and popularity. The basis of the dance is a controlled springy knee action, called the "Samba Pulse." A ballroom full of Samba dancers suggests a subdued Polka in full swing, with everyone bobbing up and down in time to the music. Integrated with this up-down movement of the legs is a swaying motion of the upper body—the "pendulum styling." The effect of this styling is that of a controlled rocking motion, one partner swaying back as the other sways forward in unison. A more advanced style of Samba employs a circling or rolling of the upper body during the execution of various step patterns. This style should not concern you as a beginner; it is only mentioned so you will recognize it when you see it. Later, when you feel sufficiently skilled, you can try to develop this technique.

Utilize the principles of the Samba Pulse and the pendulum styling while dancing the Samba. Also, make it a point to step with your foot flat, when moving either forward or backward. When stepping to the side, step on the ball of your foot. Use the straight follow-through when stepping either forward or backward, and the curved follow-through before stepping sideways. Only after you have learned the step patterns and can execute them proficiently should you study the "Astaire Styling" section of this chapter.

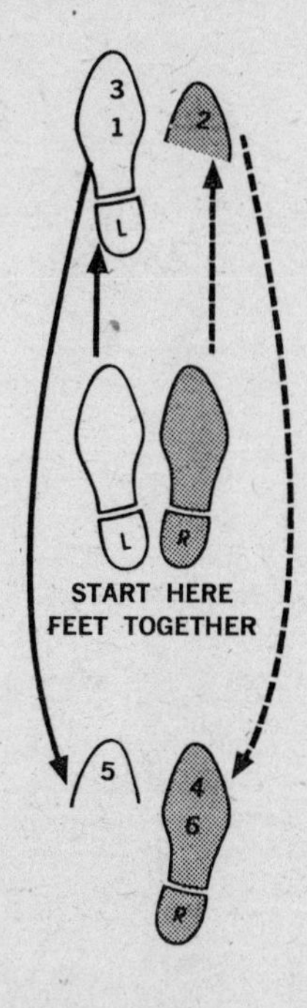

BASIC STEP

Rhythm: Quick And Quick
Quick And Quick

MAN'S PART:

1. Left foot forward, Quick, to Half Beat
2. Close with right foot, Quick, to Half Beat (put weight on ball of foot)
3. Left foot in place, Quick, to Full Beat
4. Right foot backward, Quick, to Half Beat
5. Close with left foot, Quick, to Half Beat (put weight on ball of foot)
6. Right foot in place, Quick, to Full Beat

NOTE: For a review of Quick And Quick, see Chapter 5, page 14. In all Samba patterns the 2nd and 5th steps are always taken on the ball of the foot. All other steps are taken with the foot flat. Half a foot is shown in all diagrams to signify when the ball of the foot is used.

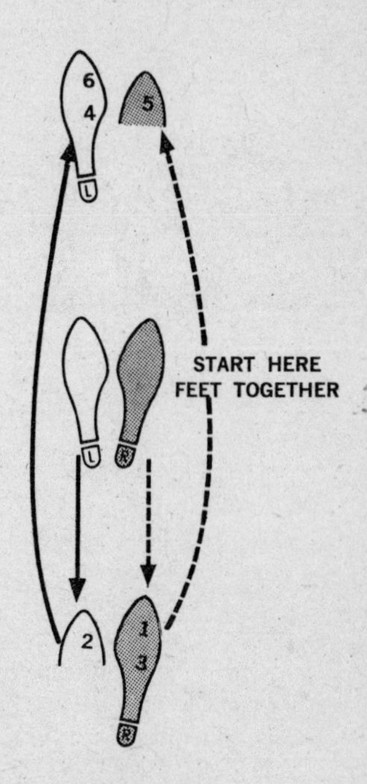

BASIC STEP

Rhythm: Quick And Quick
Quick And Quick

GIRL'S PART:

1. Right foot backward, Quick, to Half Beat
2. Close with left foot, Quick, to Half Beat (put weight on ball of foot)
3. Right foot in place, Quick, to Full Beat
4. Left foot forward, Quick, to Half Beat
5. Close with right foot, Quick, to Half Beat (put weight on ball of foot)
6. Left foot in place, Quick, to Full Beat

NOTE: See note under man's part.

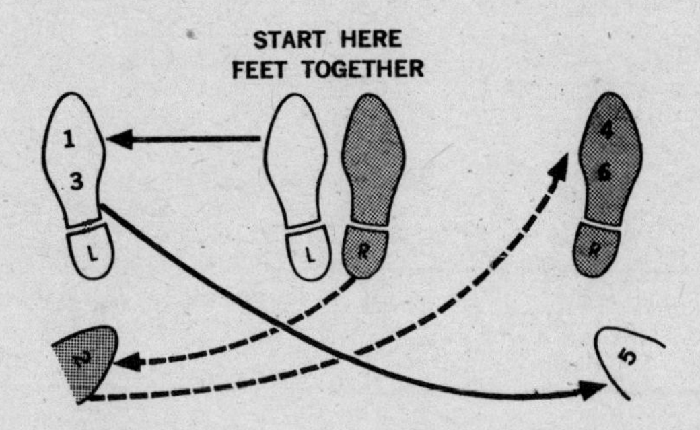

SIDE CROSS

Rhythm: Quick And Quick
Quick And Quick

MAN'S PART:

1. Left foot to side, Half beat
2. Cross right toe behind left heel, Half Beat
3. Left foot in place, Full Beat
4. Right foot to side, Half Beat
5. Cross left toe behind right heel, Half Beat
6. Right foot in place, Full Beat

NOTE: The Side Cross is similar to the Cross Balance Step in the Waltz. Maintain closed position throughout pattern.

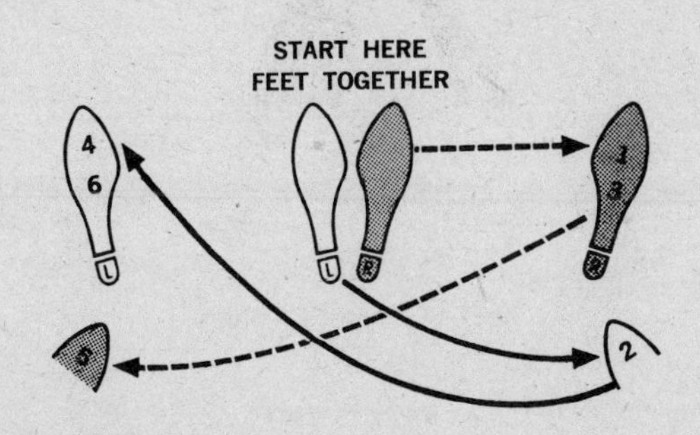

SIDE CROSS

Rhythm: Quick And Quick
Quick And Quick

GIRL'S PART:

1. Right foot to side, Half Beat
2. Cross left toe behind right heel, Half Beat
3. Right foot in place, Full Beat
4. Left foot to side, Half Beat
5. Cross right toe behind left heel, Half Beat
6. Left foot in place, Full Beat

NOTE: See note under man's part.

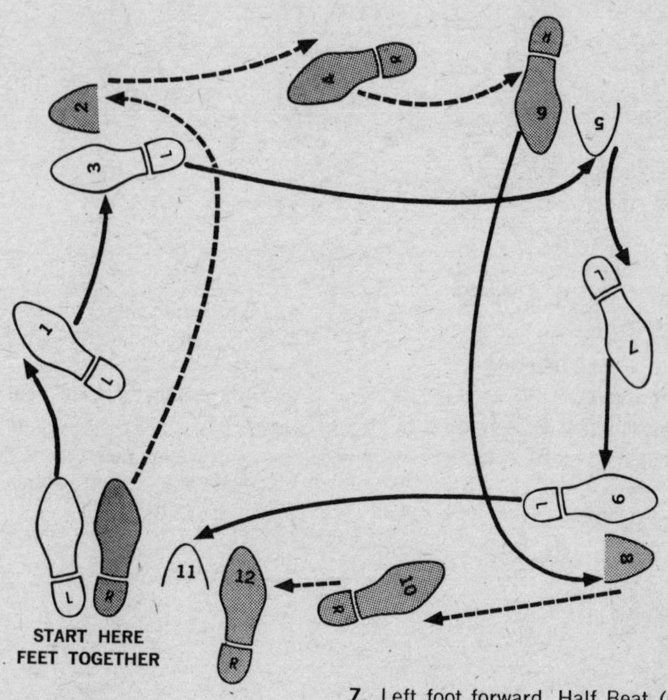

LEFT TURN

Rhythm: Quick And Quick
Quick And Quick

MAN'S PART:

1. Left foot forward, Half Beat
2. Right foot forward and to side, Half Beat (point toe to left, as shown in diagram, and step with ball of foot)
3. Close with left foot, Full Beat
4. Right foot backward, Half Beat (point toe as shown)
5. Left foot backward and to side, Half Beat (point toe as shown and step with ball of foot)
6. Close with right foot, Full Beat
7. Left foot forward, Half Beat (point toe as shown)
8. Right foot forward and to side, Half Beat (point toe as shown and step with ball of foot)
9. Close with left foot, Full Beat
10. Right foot backward, Half Beat (point toe as shown)
11. Left foot backward and to side, Half Beat (point toe as shown and step with ball of foot)
12. Close with right foot, Full Beat (turn completed)

NOTE: Turn gradually to the left, making a quarter turn between steps 1 and 3, and a quarter turn between steps 4 and 6. Then repeat.

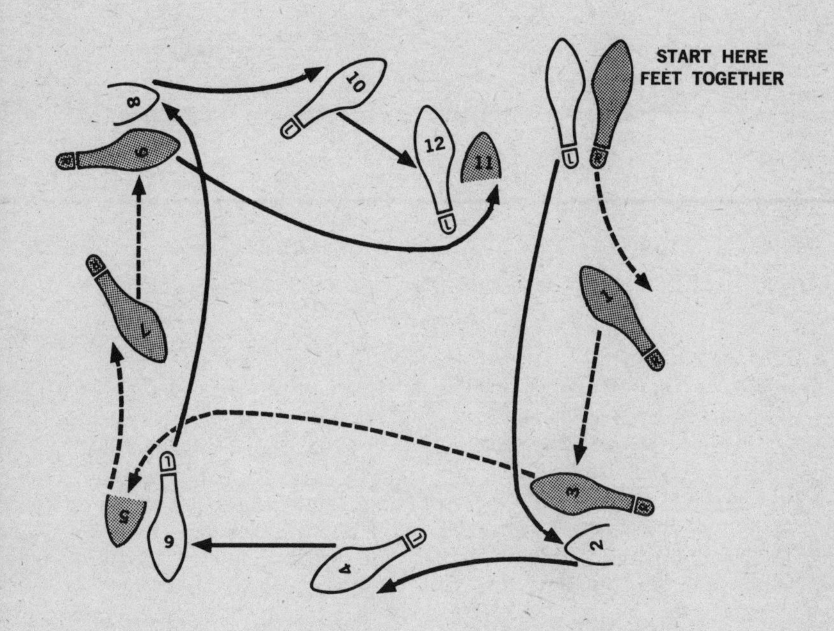

LEFT TURN

Rhythm: Quick And Quick
Quick And Quick

GIRL'S PART:

1. Right foot backward, Half Beat (point toe inward to begin turn)
2. Left foot backward and to side, Half Beat (point toe to left, as shown in diagram)
3. Close with right foot, Full Beat
4. Left foot forward, Half Beat (point toe as shown)
5. Right foot forward and to side, Half Beat (point toe as shown)
6. Close with left foot, Full Beat
7. Right foot backward, Half Beat (point toe as shown)
8. Left foot backward and to side, Half Beat (point toe as shown)
9. Close with right foot, Full Beat
10. Left foot forward, Half Beat (point toe as shown)
11. Right foot forward and to side, Half Beat (point toe as shown)
12. Close with left foot, Full Beat (turn completed)

NOTE: See note under man's part.

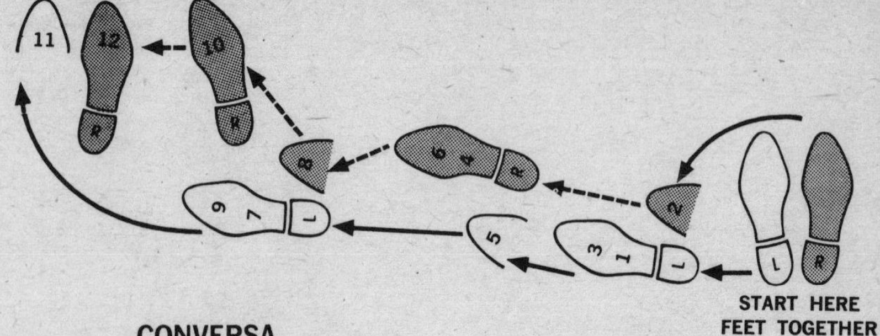

CONVERSA

Rhythm: Quick And Quick
Quick And Quick

MAN'S PART:

1. Left foot to side with toe out, Half Beat (point toe as shown in diagram)
2. Rock with right foot, Half Beat (place toe alongside left heel)
3. Left foot in place, Full Beat
4. Right foot forward, Half Beat
5. Rock with left foot, Half Beat (place toe alongside right heel)
6. Right foot in place, Full Beat
7. Left foot forward, Half Beat
8. Rock with right foot, Half Beat (place toe alongside left heel)
9. Left foot in place, Full Beat
10. Right foot forward, Half Beat (point toe as shown)
11. Left foot forward and to side, Half Beat (point toe as shown)
12. Close with right foot, Full Beat (feet together)

NOTE: The Conversa is a series of forward rocking steps danced in the left open position. Steps 1 through 10 are danced in left open position, steps 11 and 12 are danced in closed position.

CONVERSA

Rhythm: Quick And Quick
Quick And Quick

GIRL'S PART:

1. Right foot to side with toe out, Half Beat (point toe as shown)
2. Rock with left foot, Half Beat (place toe alongside right heel)
3. Right foot in place, Full Beat
4. Left foot forward, Half Beat
5. Rock with right foot, Half Beat (place toe alongside left heel)
6. Left foot in place, Full Beat
7. Right foot forward, Half Beat
8. Rock with left foot, Half Beat (place toe alongside right heel)
9. Right foot in place, Full Beat
10. Left foot forward, Half Beat (point toe as shown)
11. Right foot forward and to side, Half Beat (point toe as shown)
12. Close with left foot, Full Beat (feet together)

NOTE: See note under man's part.

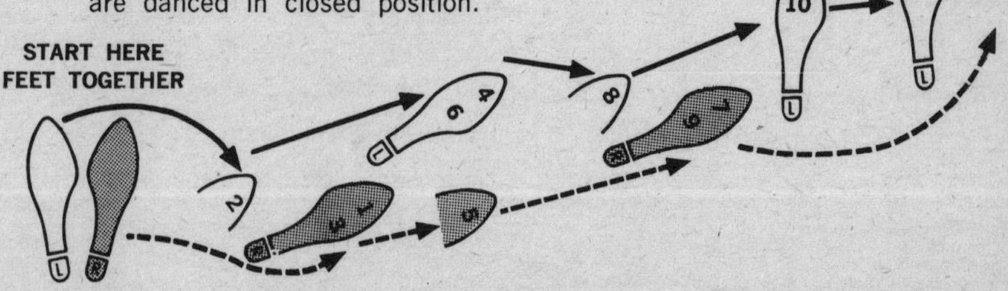

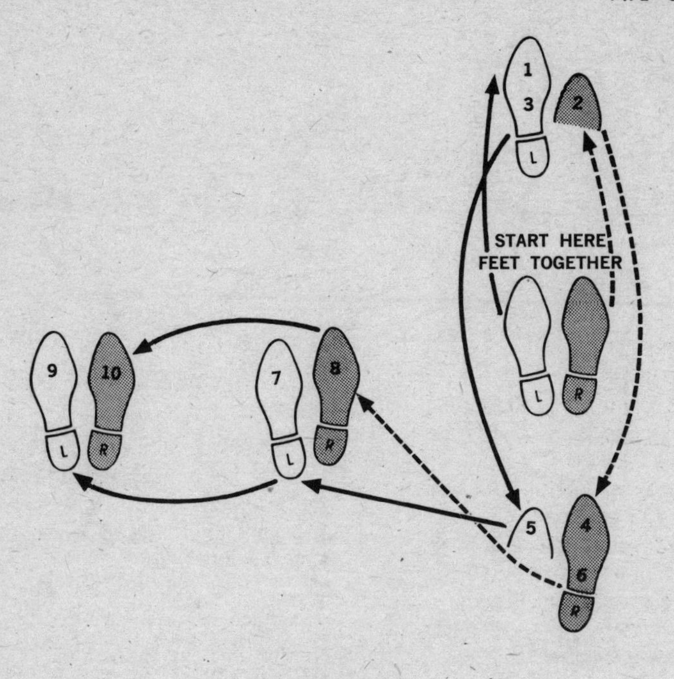

MARCHA

Rhythm: Quick And Quick
Quick And Quick
Quick, Quick
Quick, Quick

MAN'S PART:

1. Left foot forward, Half Beat
2. Close with right foot, Half Beat
3. Left foot in place, Full Beat
4. Right foot backward, Half Beat
5. Close with left foot, Half Beat
6. Right foot in place, Full Beat
7. Left foot to side, Full Beat
8. Close with right foot, Full Beat
9. Left foot to side, Full Beat
10. Close with right foot, Full Beat

NOTE: Steps 7 through 10 are danced in strict time to the music and with feet flat.

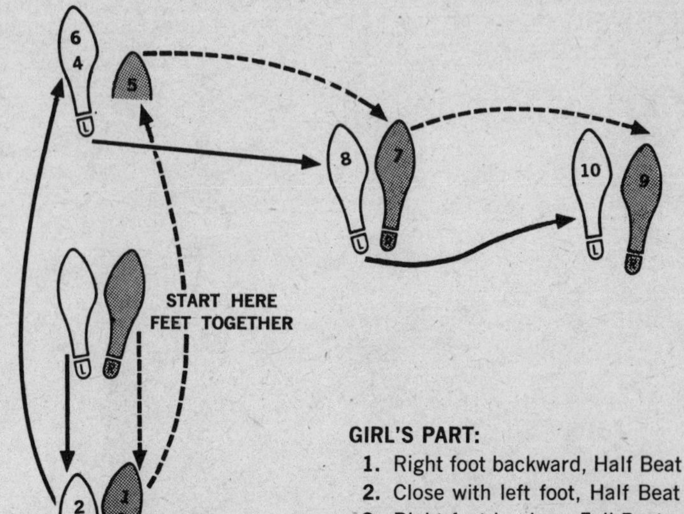

MARCHA

Rhythm: Quick And Quick
Quick And Quick
Quick, Quick
Quick, Quick

GIRL'S PART:

1. Right foot backward, Half Beat
2. Close with left foot, Half Beat
3. Right foot in place, Full Beat
4. Left foot forward, Half Beat
5. Close with right foot, Half Beat
6. Left foot in place, Full Beat
7. Right foot to side, Full Beat
8. Close with left foot, Full Beat
9. Right foot to side, Full Beat
10. Close with left foot, Full Beat

NOTE: See note under man's part.

OPEN TWINKLE

The Open Twinkle may be danced in the Samba with a slight alteration in the timing. Follow the chart below for the difference in timing:

FOX TROT	SAMBA
Slow	Quick
Quick	And
Quick	Quick
Slow	Quick
Quick	And
Quick	Quick

The footwork is the same as described in the Fox Trot (Chapter 14).

PROGRESSO

Rhythm: Quick And Quick
Quick And Quick

MAN'S PART:

1. Left foot forward, Half Beat
2. Right foot to side, Half Beat (point toe slightly inward)
3. Left foot in place, Full Beat
4. Right foot forward, Half Beat (place heel directly in front of left foot)
5. Left foot to side, Half Beat (point toe slightly inward)
6. Right foot in place, Full Beat
7. Left foot forward, Half Beat (place heel directly in front of right foot)
8. Right foot to side, Half Beat (point toe slightly inward)
9. Left foot in place, Full Beat
10. Right foot forward, Half Beat (place heel directly in front of left foot)
11. Left foot to side, Half Beat (point toe slightly inward)
12. Right foot in place, Full Beat

NOTE: As the man dances the Progresso forward, the girl is, in effect, dancing the Side Cross. (See drawings.)

STEPS 1 and 7

STEPS 2 and 3, 8 and 9

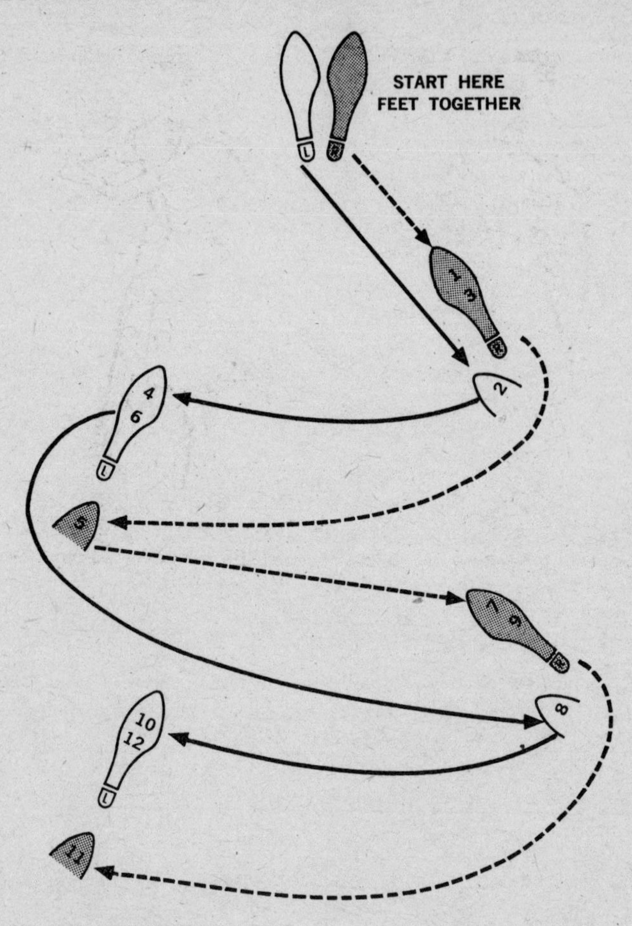

PROGRESSO

Rhythm: Quick And Quick
Quick And Quick

GIRL'S PART:

1. Right foot backward diagonal, Half Beat
2. Cross left foot behind right foot, Half Beat
3. Right foot in place, Full Beat
4. Left foot backward diagonal, Half Beat
5. Cross right foot behind left foot, Half Beat
6. Left foot in place, Full Beat
7. Right foot backward diagonal, Half Beat
8. Cross left foot behind right foot, Half Beat
9. Right foot in place, Full Beat
10. Left foot backward diagonal, Half Beat
11. Cross right foot behind left foot, Half Beat
12. Left foot in place, Full Beat

NOTE: See note under man's part.

STEPS 4 and 10

STEPS 5 and 6, 11 and 12

Astaire Styling: The Samba

The two techniques which give the Samba its characteristic flavor and style—the up and down action of the knees, and the forward and back sway of the upper part of the body—are performed simultaneously when dancing with a partner, but you should learn them separately at first. Do not overdo the Samba Pulse while you are learning or you'll tire very quickly and find the Samba a chore rather than a joy.

To do the Samba Pulse:

1. Start with your feet together.

2. Bend both knees in a downward direction, keeping your feet flat.

3. Straighten both knees.

4. Repeat.

When you bend your knees, count "Quick." When you straighten your knees, count "And." Continue repeating the Pulse, counting "Quick, And, Quick, And, Quick, And," etc. Notice that the accent of stress is on the downward or bending action rather than on the upward or straightening action. Dance the Pulse a few more times at a faster tempo, subduing the knee action.

Now apply the Samba Pulse to the Basic Step, as follows:

1. Start with your feet together, and let the pulse action in your knees begin without taking any steps. Count "Quick, And, Quick, And," at the same time.

2. Step forward with the left foot (the girl, of course, steps backward with her right foot and applies all directions to her own part). At the same time, bend both knees and count "Quick."

3. Close the right foot to the left foot. At the same time, straighten both knees and count "And."

4. Step in place with the left foot. At the same time, bend both knees and count "Quick."

5. Now straighten both knees and count "And," but don't take any steps.

6. Step backward with the right foot. At the same time, bend both knees and count "Quick."

7. Close the left foot to the right foot. At the same time, straighten both knees and count "And."

8. Step in place with the right foot. At the same time, bend both knees and count "Quick."

9. Now straighten both knees and count "And," but don't take any steps.

Continue repeating the Basic Step, starting from step 2 each time. Try it to the music only after you can do each movement comfortably.

When you think you've mastered the Samba Pulse, add the pendulum styling—the back-and-forth sway of your upper body. The idea is to move the top half of your body in opposition to the leg that is in motion. This means that when you step forward, your body sways slightly backward; when you step backward, your body sways slightly forward. The effect is that of a pendulum, swinging in time to the tick-tock of a clock.

SAMBA COMBINATIONS

Pattern	Number of Steps	Rhythm
(A)		
Basic Step	6	
Side Cross	6	All steps: Quick And Quick
Conversa	12	
(B)		
Left Turn	12	Quick And Quick
Basic Step	6	Quick And Quick
Marcha	4	Quick, Quick, Quick, Quick
(C)		
Basic Step	6	
Progresso	12	All steps: Quick And Quick
Basic Step	6	

CHAPTER TWENTY-TWO

The Merengue

INTRODUCTION

BOTH Haiti and the Dominican Republic claim that the Merengue originated in their country. According to the Haitians an early ruler of their country had a lame son who liked to dance. In order that this beloved prince would not feel self-conscious about his affliction, the entire populace took to dancing as though all were lame. The Dominicans tell how the dance originated at a fiesta that was given to honor a returning war hero. When the brave warrior rose to dance, he limped on his wounded left leg. Rather than make him feel at a disadvantage, all the men present also favored their left legs on the dance floor.

As you can infer from these stories, a unique characteristic of the Merengue is a step which appears to be taken with a slight limp—though it is not really a limp. The man steps with his left leg, and the girl with her right leg, flexing the knee a bit more than usual and at the same time leaning the body slightly to the same side. Except for this singular difference, the Merengue is danced with much the same motion as the Rumba and Mambo, utilizing the Cuban hip movement. See the "Astaire Styling" section at the end of this chapter for more detailed instruction.

Haitians and Dominicans alike refer to the Merengue as their "singing dance." This is understandable when you consider the exhilarating brightness of the staccato rhythm. There is nothing monotonous or routine about the Merengue, yet the beginner generally has very little trouble learning the mechanics. A minimum of technique is essential. Make your steps as neat and punctual as possible, taking one step to each beat of music. There are no two-beat steps included in the following patterns. Except for the Double Chassé, the diagrams should all be stepped through to the same even tempo. All the steps are Quick steps, with the accent on the odd count: "One, Two, THREE, Four."

You'll find the Merengue easy to master and lots of fun.

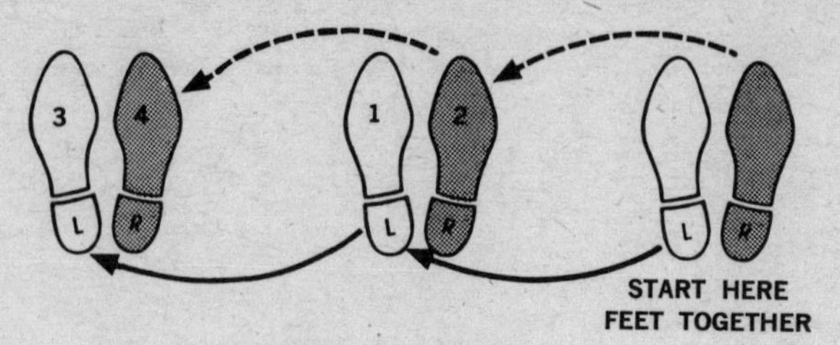

BASIC CHASSÉ

Count: One, Two, THREE, Four

MAN'S PART:

1. Left foot to side
2. Close with right foot
3. Left foot to side
4. Close with right foot

NOTE: All steps in the Merengue are Quick, one step to each beat of music; therefore, the "Quick" will not be indicated in the step diagrams that follow in this chapter. Accent the 1st and 3rd steps by flexing the knee slightly.

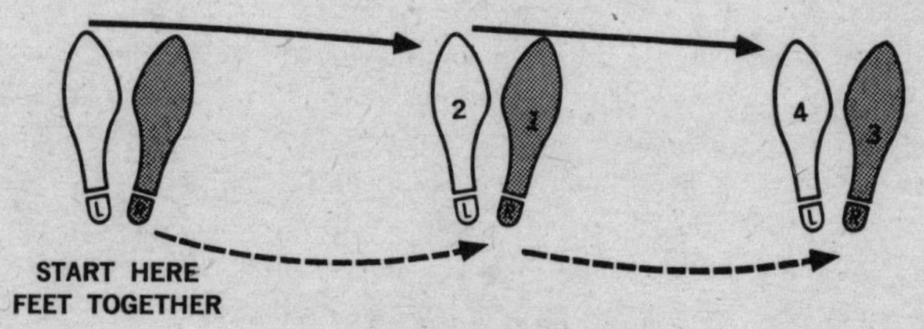

BASIC CHASSÉ

Count: One, Two, THREE, Four

GIRL'S PART:

1. Right foot to side
2. Close with left foot
3. Right foot to side
4. Close with left foot

NOTE: See note under man's part.

THE CUADRO

Count: One, Two, THREE, Four
One, Two, THREE, Four

MAN'S PART:

1. Left foot to side
2. Close with right foot
3. Left foot forward
4. Right foot to side
5. Close with left foot
6. Right foot backward
7. Left foot to side
8. Close with right foot

NOTE: The Cuadro (Box Step) may be danced squarely, as illustrated, or may be danced turning to the left, as in the Left Turn in the Fox Trot or Waltz.

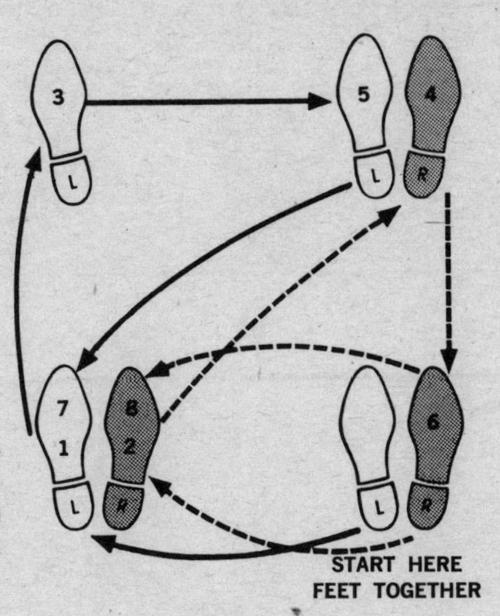

THE CUADRO

Count: One, Two, THREE, Four
One, Two, THREE, Four

GIRL'S PART:

1. Right foot to side
2. Close with left foot
3. Right foot backward
4. Left foot to side
5. Close with right foot
6. Left foot forward
7. Right foot to side
8. Close with left foot

NOTE: See note under man's part.

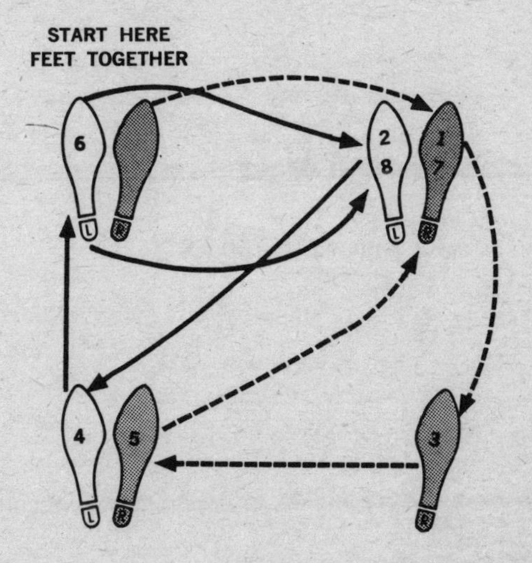

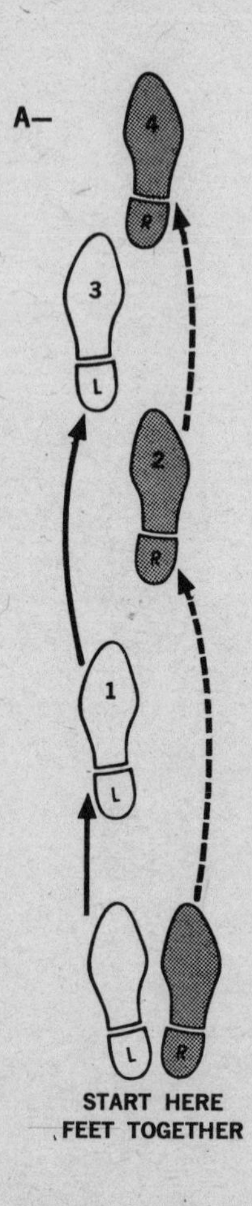

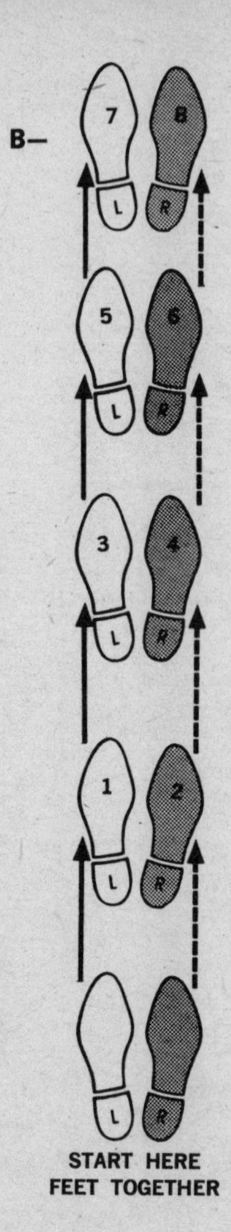

DOMINICAN WALKS

Count: One, Two, THREE, Four
One, Two, THREE, Four

MAN'S PART: Forward (A)

1. Left foot forward
2. Right foot forward
3. Left foot forward
4. Right foot forward

5.–8. Repeat

MAN'S PART: Forward (B)

1. Left foot forward
2. Close with right foot
3. Left foot forward
4. Close with right foot

5.–8. Repeat

NOTE: The man should learn to do this step in both forward and backward directions. This pattern may be danced squarely, as illustrated, or turning to the left, as in the Running Steps in the Waltz.

START HERE
FEET TOGETHER

A—

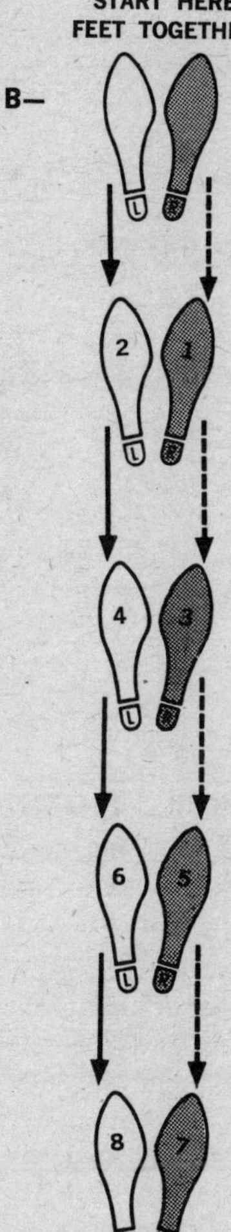

DOMINICAN WALKS

Count: One, Two, THREE, Four
One, Two, THREE, Four

GIRL'S PART: Backward (A)

1. Right foot backward
2. Left foot backward
3. Right foot backward
4. Left foot backward

5.—8. Repeat

GIRL'S PART: Backward (B)

1. Right foot backward
2. Close with left foot
3. Right foot backward
4. Close with left foot

5.—8. Repeat

NOTE: The girl should learn to do this step in both forward and backward directions. See note under man's part.

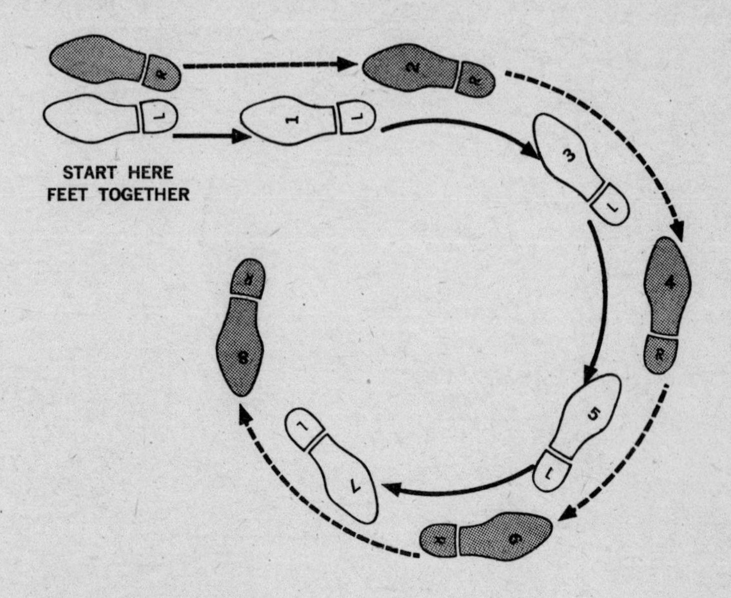

DOMINICAN TURN

Count: One, Two, THREE, Four
One, Two, THREE, Four

MAN'S PART:

1. Left foot backward
2. Right foot backward
3. Left foot backward (point toe to begin turn, as shown in diagram)
4. Right foot backward (point toe as shown)
5. Left foot backward (point toe as shown)
6. Right foot backward (point toe as shown)
7. Left foot backward (point toe as shown)
8. Right foot backward (point toe as shown)

NOTE: The Dominican Turn is danced backward, turning to the right. For the most attractive appearance, take small steps, keeping the circle as compact as possible.

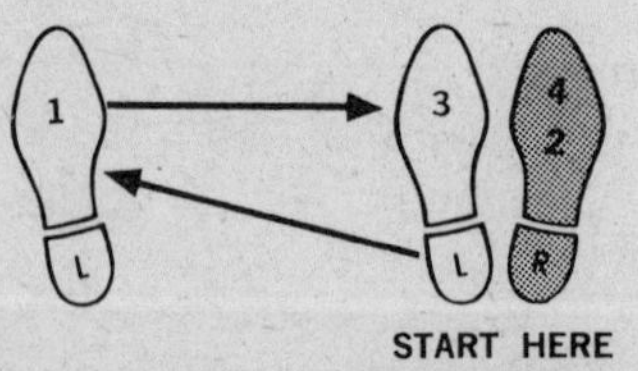

DOMINICAN SIDE BREAK

Count: One, Two, THREE, Four

MAN'S PART:

1. Left foot to side
2. Right foot in place
3. Close with left
4. Right foot in place

NOTE: Accent the first step to side by flexing knee.

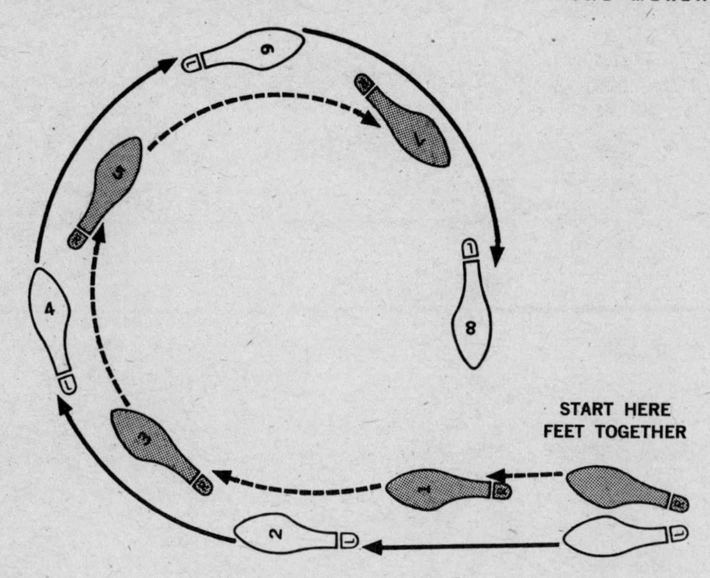

DOMINICAN TURN

Count: One, Two, THREE, Four
One, Two, THREE, Four

GIRL'S PART:

1. Right foot forward
2. Left foot forward
3. Right foot forward (point toe to begin turn, as shown in diagram)
4. Left foot forward (point toe as shown)
5. Right foot forward (point toe as shown)
6. Left foot forward (point toe as shown)
7. Right foot forward (point toe as shown)
8. Left foot forward (point toe as shown)

NOTE: The Dominican Turn is danced forward, turning to the right. For the most attractive appearance, take small steps, keeping the circle as compact as possible.

DOMINICAN SIDE BREAK

Count: One, Two, THREE, Four

GIRL'S PART:

1. Right foot to side
2. Left foot in place
3. Close with right foot
4. Left foot in place

NOTE: See note under man's part.

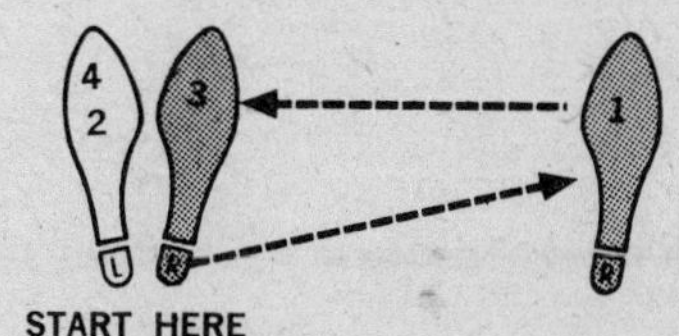

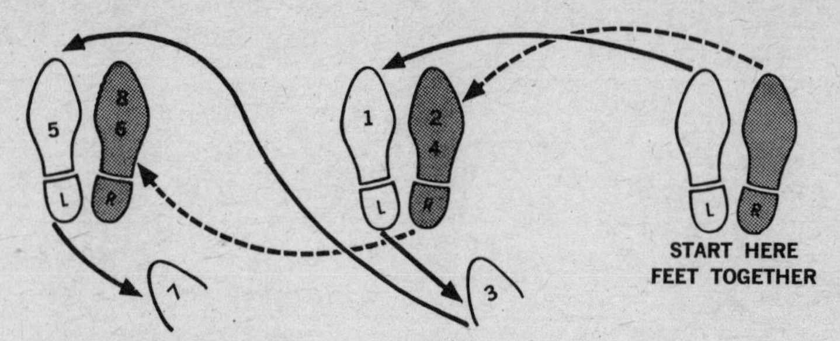

LEFT OPEN BREAK

Count: One, Two, THREE, Four
One, Two, THREE, Four

MAN'S PART:

1. Left foot to side
2. Close with right foot
3. Left foot backward (cross behind right foot, putting weight on ball of left foot)
4. Right foot in place
5. Left foot to side
6. Close with right foot
7. Left foot backward (cross behind right foot, putting weight on ball of left foot)
8. Right foot in place

NOTE: As the feet close (the 2nd and 6th steps) the man leads his partner to face in the left open position. Steps 3 and 7 are danced in the left open position. (See drawings.)

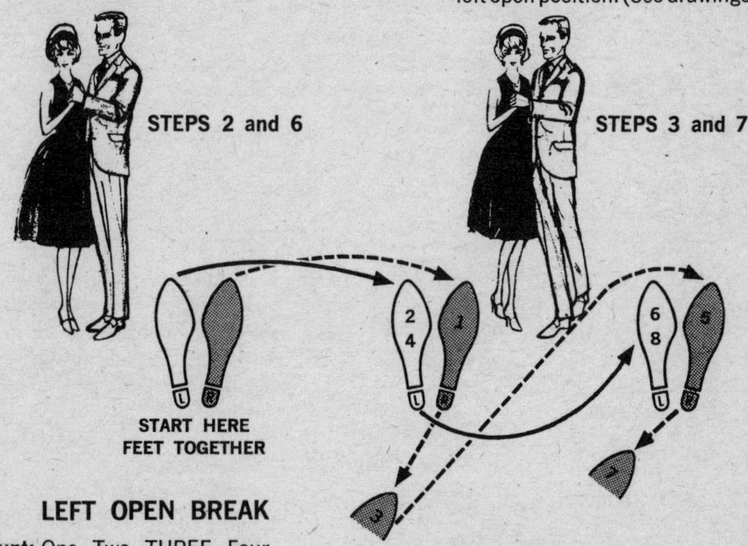

LEFT OPEN BREAK

Count: One, Two, THREE, Four
One, Two, THREE, Four

GIRL'S PART:

1. Right foot to side
2. Close with left foot
3. Right foot backward (cross behind left foot, putting weight on ball of right foot)
4. Left foot in place
5. Right foot to side
6. Close with left foot
7. Right foot backward (cross behind left foot, putting weight on ball of right foot)
8. Left foot in place

NOTE: See note under man's part.

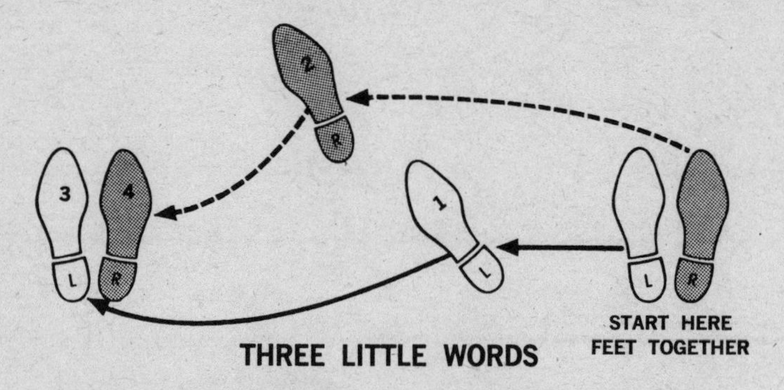

THREE LITTLE WORDS

Count: One, Two, THREE, Four

MAN'S PART:

1. Left foot to side (point toe as shown in diagram)
2. Right foot forward (cross in front of left foot, pointing toe as shown)
3. Left foot to side
4. Close with right foot

NOTE: The 1st and 2nd steps are danced in the left open position. The 3rd and 4th steps are danced in closed position.

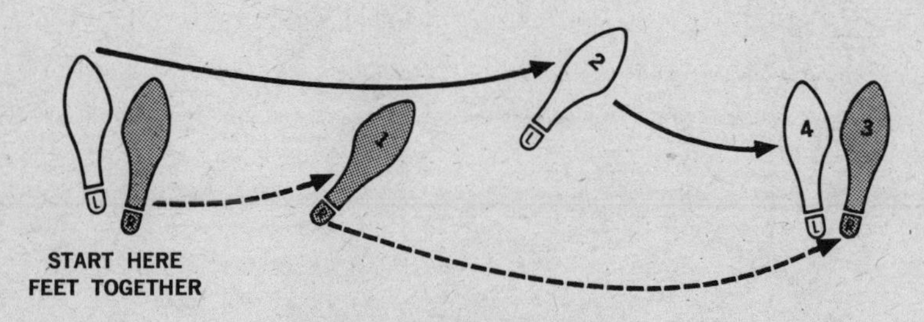

THREE LITTLE WORDS

Count: One, Two, THREE, Four

GIRL'S PART:

1. Right foot to side (point toe as shown in diagram)
2. Left foot forward (cross in front of right foot, pointing toe as shown)
3. Right foot to side
4. Close with left foot

NOTE: See note under man's part.

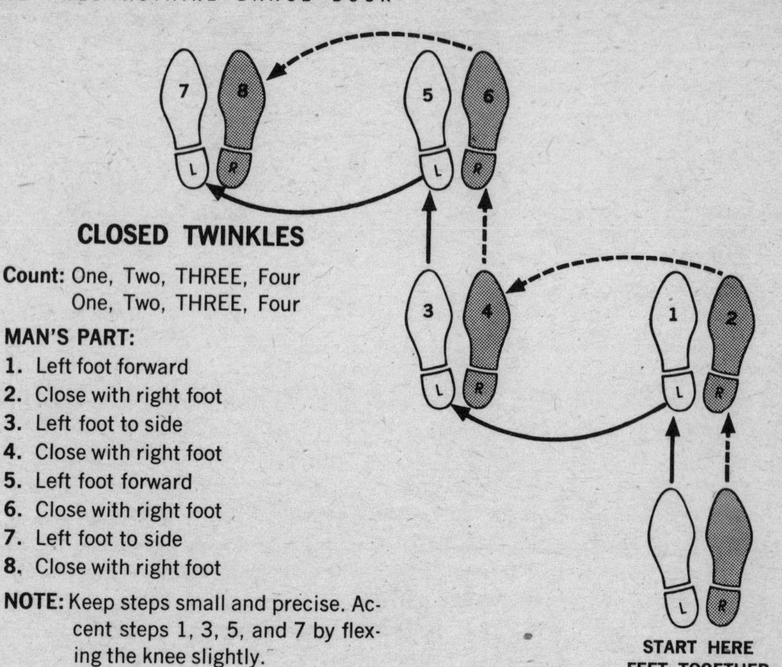

CLOSED TWINKLES

Count: One, Two, THREE, Four
One, Two, THREE, Four

MAN'S PART:

1. Left foot forward
2. Close with right foot
3. Left foot to side
4. Close with right foot
5. Left foot forward
6. Close with right foot
7. Left foot to side
8. Close with right foot

NOTE: Keep steps small and precise. Accent steps 1, 3, 5, and 7 by flexing the knee slightly.

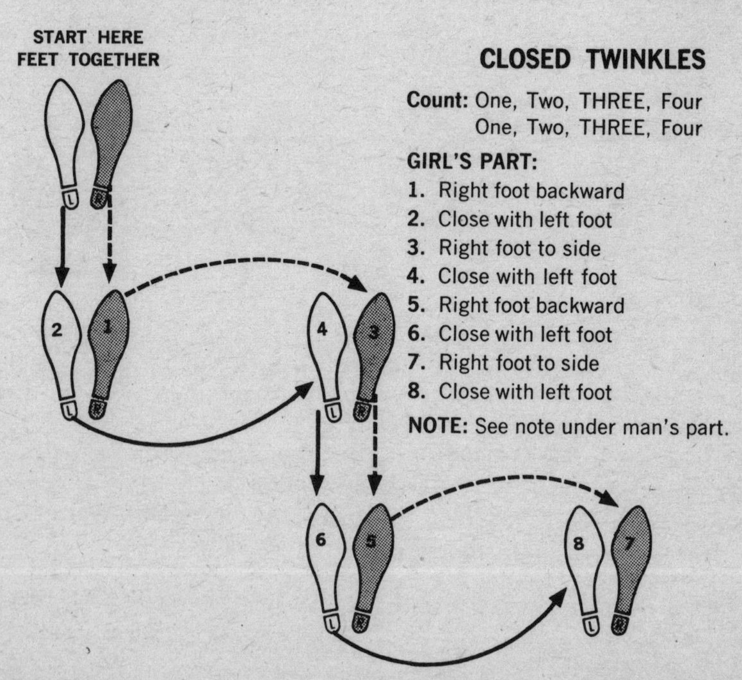

CLOSED TWINKLES

Count: One, Two, THREE, Four
One, Two, THREE, Four

GIRL'S PART:

1. Right foot backward
2. Close with left foot
3. Right foot to side
4. Close with left foot
5. Right foot backward
6. Close with left foot
7. Right foot to side
8. Close with left foot

NOTE: See note under man's part.

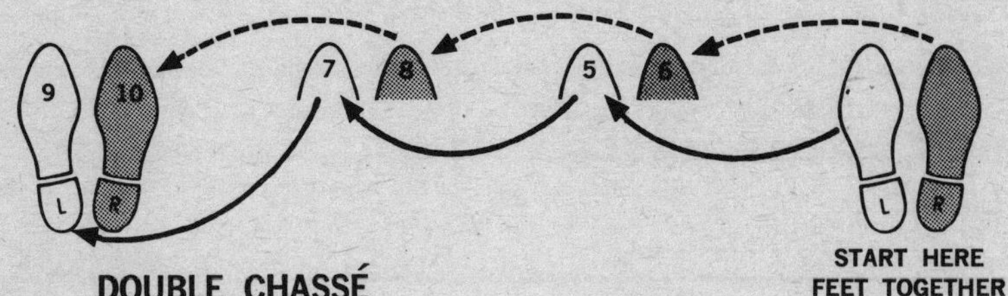

DOUBLE CHASSÉ

Count: One, Two, THREE, Four
Five And Six And Seven, Eight

MAN'S PART:

1.—4. Same as in Basic Chassé
5. Left foot to side, Half Beat (take step on ball of foot)
6. Close with right foot, Half Beat (on ball of foot)
7. Left foot to side, Half Beat (on ball of foot)
8. Close with right foot, Half Beat (on ball of foot)
9. Left foot to side, Full Beat
10. Close with right foot, Full Beat

NOTE: Steps 5, 6, 7, and 8 are taken only on the balls of the feet. The timing of these four steps is twice as fast as the normal timing in the Merengue.

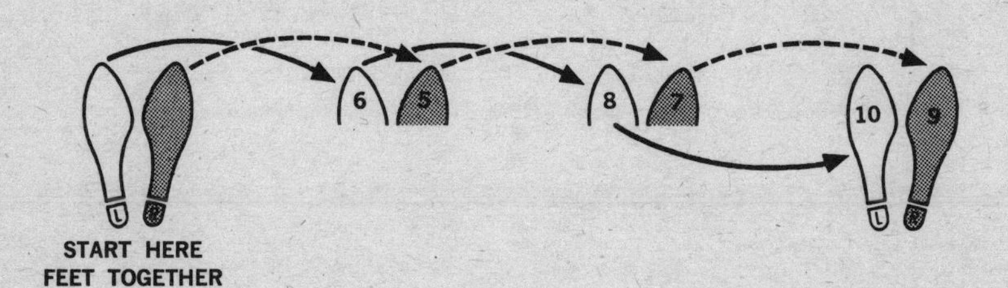

DOUBLE CHASSÉ

Count: One, Two, THREE, Four
Five And Six And Seven, Eight

GIRL'S PART:

1.—4. Same as in Basic Chassé
5. Right foot to side, Half Beat (take step on ball of foot)
6. Close with left foot, Half Beat (on ball of foot)
7. Right foot to side, Half Beat (on ball of foot)
8. Close with left foot, Half Beat (on ball of foot)
9. Right foot to side, Full Beat
10. Close with left foot, Full Beat

NOTE: See note under man's part.

Astaire Styling: The Merengue

Once you have learned the simple step patterns of the Merengue, one task remains, and that is to add the proper body motion. First, consider your hip motion. It is the same Cuban motion that you learned in the Rumba, Mambo, and Cha Cha Cha. All you have to do is to tailor it to the Merengue rhythm and tempo, then concentrate on diminishing the side-to-side hip swing until it is barely discernible.

Second, there is the characteristic limping motion on the first or third step of each sequence. Beware of a natural tendency to overdo it. Simply flex your knee a bit farther than usual and simultaneously lean your body slightly in the same direction. The man will always execute this motion with his left leg; the girl with her right leg. This Merengue "limp" should be done quickly and smartly, in accordance with the music.

Practice the Astaire Styling in place to music, then go back through all the step patterns and add the proper body motion.

MERENGUE COMBINATIONS

Pattern	Number of Steps	Rhythm
(A)		
Basic Chassé	4	
The Cuadro	8	All steps: Quick, Quick, Quick, Quick
Closed Twinkles	8	
(B)		
Double Chassé	10	Quick, Quick, Quick, Quick, Quick And Quick And Quick, Quick
Dominican Walks—Forward	8	Quick, Quick, Quick, Quick
Basic Chassé	4	Quick, Quick, Quick, Quick
(C)		
Dominican Side Break	4	
Left Open Break	4	All steps: Quick, Quick, Quick, Quick
Dominican Turn	8	
Basic Chassé	4	

CHAPTER TWENTY-THREE

The Polka

INTRODUCTION

THE Polka is thought to be of Bohemian origin. In its original form it was a "round dance," that is, it was danced by several couples together. Toward the middle of the last century it emerged as a dance for two partners and its popularity spread rapidly. The foot-tapping, hand-clapping melodies of the Polka were soon heard across the entire European continent.

Each country immediately put its own stamp on the dance. Americans have demonstrated a marked preference for the Polish form of the Polka, which is very similar to the original Bohemian folk dance. In Poland today, the Polka is ranked as the national dance. Indeed, we owe our thanks to the generation of Polish immigrants that brought the Polka to our country.

As you work with the notes and diagrams, you will see that all patterns are scored without the standard hop-steps that are common in the Polka. These were omitted to avoid confusion. When learning a pattern, it is first of all necessary to know the sequence of steps and the direction in which you are going; then you may add the hop-steps in this manner: If the step pattern is:

1. Left foot forward, Quick
2. Close with right foot, Quick
3. Left foot forward, Slow

hop on the right foot a fraction of a beat before the first step. If the pattern begins on the right foot, hop on the left foot a fraction of a beat before the first step. This, of course, will alter the rhythm slightly. Instead of counting "Quick, Quick, Slow," you will count "And Quick, Quick, Slow." The "And," as you already know, represents a half-beat step.

START HERE
FEET TOGETHER

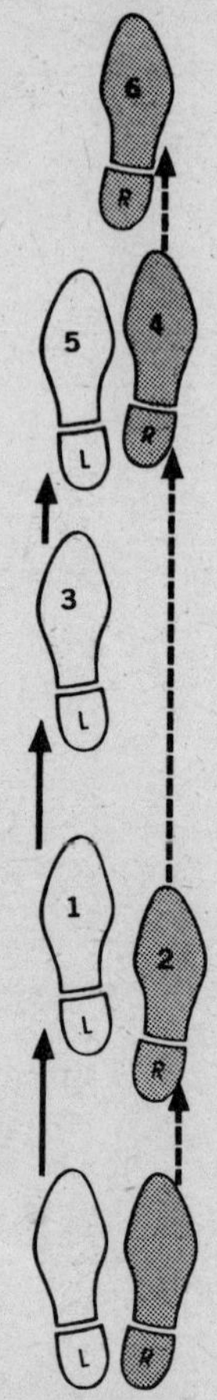

START HERE
FEET TOGETHER

BASIC FORWARD STEP

Rhythm: Quick, Quick, Slow
Quick, Quick, Slow

MAN'S PART:

1. Left foot forward, Quick
2. Close with right foot, Quick
3. Left foot forward, Slow
4. Right foot forward, Quick
5. Close with left foot, Quick
6. Right foot forward, Slow

NOTE: Take small steps throughout the Polka. Maintain closed position, or place both hands on partner's shoulders.

BASIC BACKWARD STEP

Rhythm: Quick, Quick, Slow
Quick, Quick, Slow

GIRL'S PART:

1. Right foot backward, Quick
2. Close with left foot, Quick
3. Right foot backward, Slow
4. Left foot backward, Quick
5. Close with right foot, Quick
6. Left foot backward, Slow

NOTE: See note under man's part.

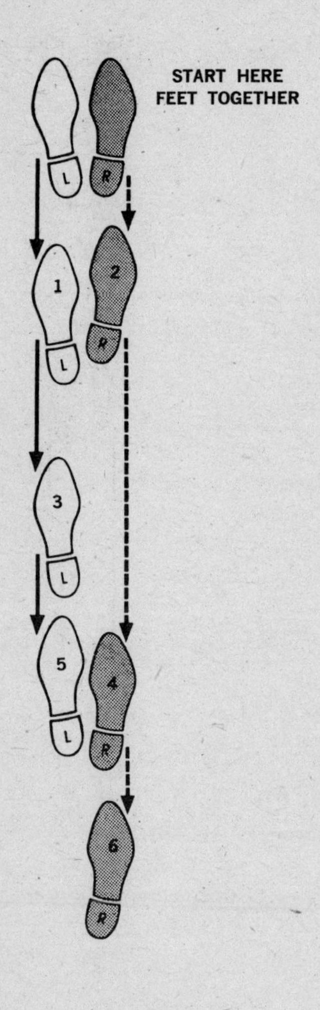

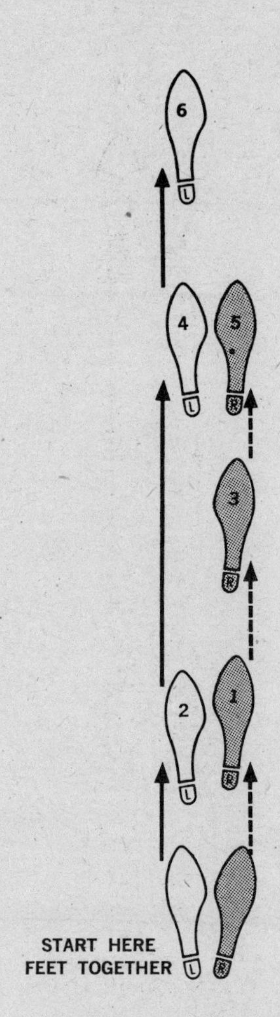

BASIC BACKWARD STEP

Rhythm: Quick, Quick, Slow
Quick, Quick, Slow

MAN'S PART:

1. Left foot backward, Quick
2. Close with right foot, Quick
3. Left foot backward, Slow
4. Right foot backward, Quick
5. Close with left foot, Quick
6. Right foot backward, Slow

BASIC FORWARD STEP

Rhythm: Quick, Quick, Slow
Quick, Quick, Slow

GIRL'S PART:

1. Right foot forward, Quick
2. Close with left foot, Quick
3. Right foot forward, Slow
4. Left foot forward, Quick
5. Close with right foot, Quick
6. Left foot forward, Slow

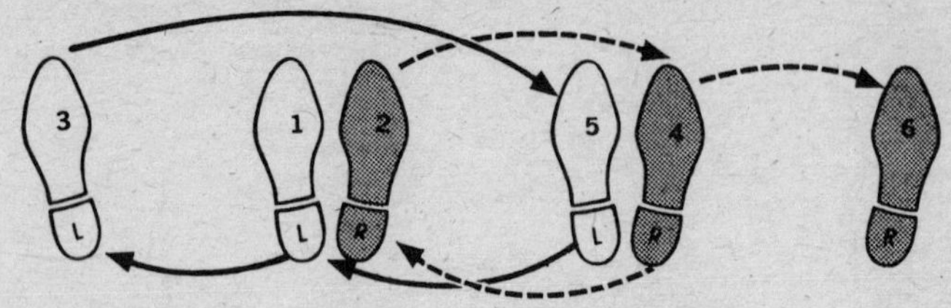

BASIC SIDE STEP

Rhythm: Quick, Quick, Slow
Quick, Quick, Slow

MAN'S PART:

1. Left foot to side, Quick
2. Close with right foot, Quick
3. Left foot to side, Slow
4. Right foot to right side, Quick
5. Close with left foot, Quick
6. Right foot to side, Slow

NOTE: The Basic Side Step is danced in a small area. It is used when progression is blocked by another couple.

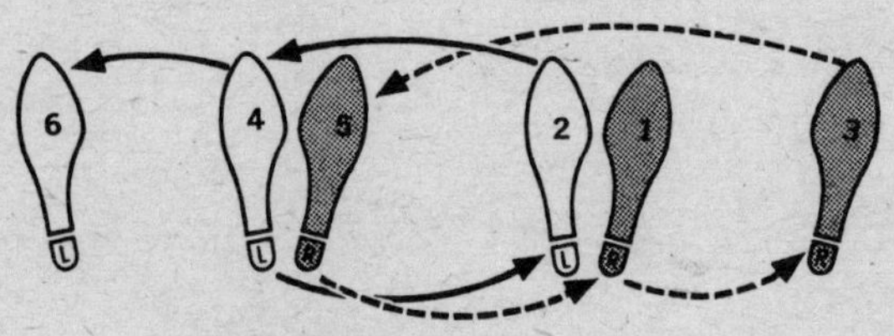

BASIC SIDE STEP

Rhythm: Quick, Quick, Slow
Quick, Quick, Slow

GIRL'S PART:

1. Right foot to side, Quick
2. Close with left foot, Quick
3. Right foot to side, Slow
4. Left foot to left side, Quick
5. Close with right foot, Quick
6. Left foot to side, Slow

NOTE: See note under man's part.

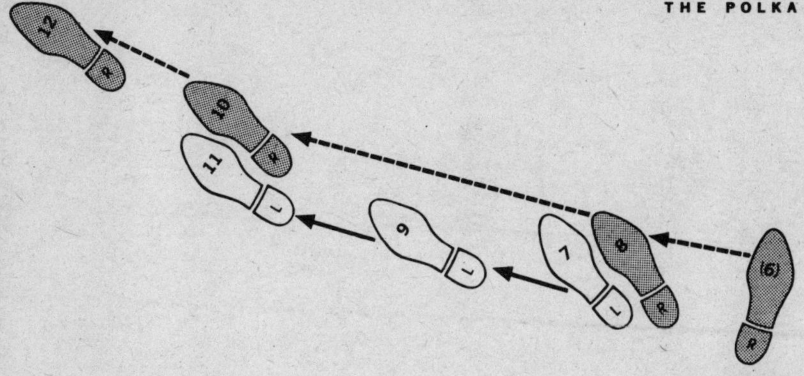

START HERE

OPEN TRAVEL STEP

Rhythm: Quick, Quick, Slow
Quick, Quick, Slow

MAN'S PART:

1.–6. Same as Basic Side Step
7. Left foot in place, Quick (point toe as shown in diagram)
8. Close with right foot, Quick
9. Left foot forward, Slow
10. Right foot forward, Quick
11. Close with left foot, Quick
12. Right foot forward, Slow

NOTE: After dancing the six steps of the Basic Side Step, turn slightly to face in left open position and continue dancing the Open Travel Step. For added style, the man may release his left hand hold in left open position. After the 12th step you may either repeat the pattern from step 7 or return to closed position and dance the Basic Side Step.

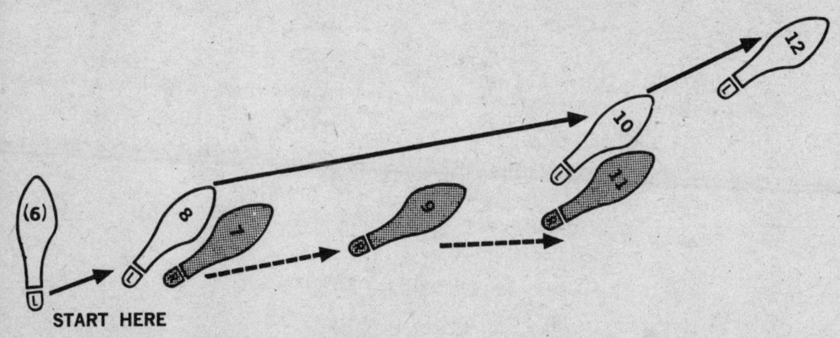

START HERE

OPEN TRAVEL STEP

Rhythm: Quick, Quick, Slow
Quick, Quick, Slow

GIRL'S PART:

1.–6. Same as Basic Side Step
7. Right foot in place, Quick (point toe as shown in diagram)
8. Close with left foot, Quick
9. Right foot forward, Slow
10. Left foot forward, Quick
11. Close with right foot, Quick
12. Left foot forward, Slow

NOTE: See note under man's part.

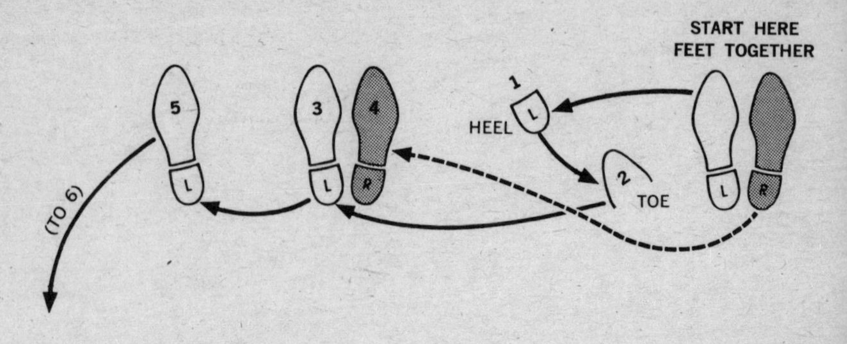

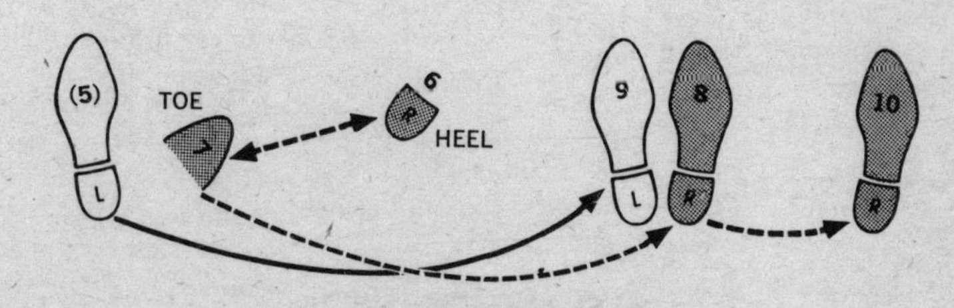

HEEL-AND-TOE BREAK

Rhythm: Slow, Slow, Quick, Quick, Slow
Slow, Slow, Quick, Quick, Slow

MAN'S PART:

1. Left heel to side, Slow (touch heel to floor, keeping weight on right leg)
2. Tap left toe, Slow (still keep weight on right leg)
3. Left foot to side, Quick
4. Close with right foot, Quick
5. Left foot to side, Slow
6. Right heel to side, Slow (touch heel to floor, keeping weight on left foot)
7. Tap right toe, Slow (keep weight still on left leg)
8. Right foot to side, Quick
9. Close with left foot, Quick
10. Right foot to side, Slow

NOTE: The Heel-and-Toe Break is similar to the Heel and Toe in the Cha Cha Cha. No weight is applied to the heel and toe movements.

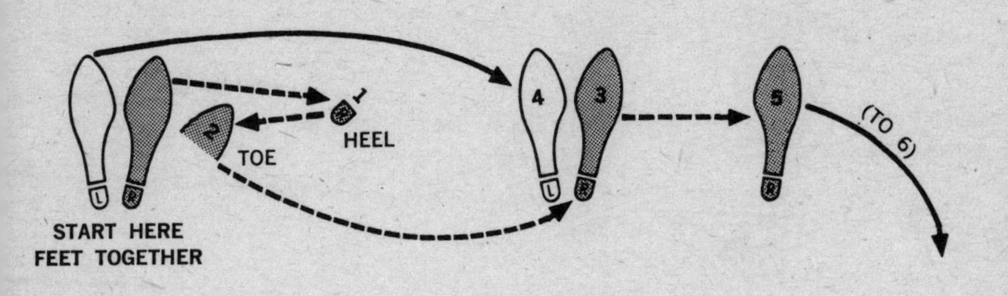

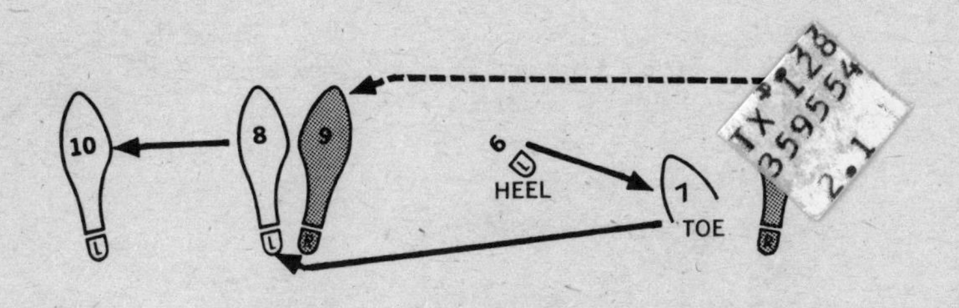

HEEL-AND-TOE BREAK

Rhythm: Slow, Slow, Quick, Quick, Slow
Slow, Slow, Quick, Quick, Slow

GIRL'S PART:

1. Right heel to side, Slow (touch heel to floor, keeping weight on left leg)
2. Tap right toe, Slow (keep weight still on left leg)
3. Right foot to side, Quick
4. Close with left foot, Quick
5. Right foot to side, Slow
6. Left heel to side, Slow (touch heel to floor, keeping weight on right leg)
7. Tap left toe, Slow (keep weight still on right leg)
8. Left foot to side, Quick
9. Close with right foot, Quick
10. Left foot to side, Slow

NOTE: See note under man's part.

Astaire Styling: The Polka

The Polka is danced with a light, bouncy quality. Your dancing should look as effortless as possible. When doing any of the hop-steps be careful not to spring off the floor with wild abandon; hop airily and gracefully.

When moving sideways, sway the upper part of your body in the direction you are traveling. This rhythmic body sway gives the Polka a polished appearance that is extremely pleasing to the eye. It also accentuates the dancer's feeling of grace and coordination.

If you wish to enlarge your repertoire of Polka steps, the following patterns can easily be adapted from the Fox Trot—the Left Turn and Right Turn; from the Rumba—the Side Break, Forward Rock, and Backward Rock.

Refer back to the notes and diagrams in the Fox Trot and Rumba lessons (Chapters 14 and 19). Do not alter the timing or rhythm, but dance the patterns just twice as fast. For the Rumba steps, eliminate the Cuban styling.

POLKA COMBINATIONS

Pattern	Number of Steps	Rhythm
(A)		
Basic Forward Step	6	
Basic Side Step	6	All steps: Quick, Quick, Slow
Open Travel Step	12	
Basic Side Step	6	
(B)		
Basic Side Step	6	Quick, Quick, Slow
Left Turn	12	See Left Turn in Fox Trot, Chapter 14
Heel-and-Toe Break	10	Slow, Slow, Quick, Quick, Slow
Basic Side Step	6	Quick, Quick, Slow